The Trick to Money Is Having Some!

BY STUART WILDE

BOOKS

THE TAOS QUINTET:
Affirmations
The Force
Miracles
The Quickening
The Trick to Money Is Having Some!

Infinite Self: 33 Steps to Reclaiming Your Inner Power
"Life Was Never Meant to Be a Struggle"
The Secrets of Life
Silent Power
Weight Loss for the Mind
Whispering Winds of Change

AUDIOCASSETTES

The Art of Meditation
Silent Power (audio book)
The Force (audio book)
Miracles (audio book)
Happiness Is Your Destiny
Intuition
Loving Relationships

Available at your local bookstore, or call **(800) 654-5126**

Please visit the Hay House Website at: **www.hayhouse.com** and
Stuart Wilde's Website at: **www.powersource.com/wilde**

The Trick to Money Is Having Some!

STUART WILDE

Hay House, Inc.
Carlsbad, CA

Published and distributed in the United States by:
Hay House, Inc., P.O. Box 5100, Carlsbad, CA 92018-5100
(800) 654-5126 • (800) 650-5115 (fax)

Designed by: Jenny Richards

Library of Congress Cataloging-in-Publication Data

Wilde, Stuart, 1946–
　　The trick to money is having some! / Stuart Wilde.
　　　　p.　　cm.
　　Originally published: Taos, N.M.: White Dove International, 1989.
　　ISBN 1-56170-168-8 (tradepaper)
　　1. Finance, Personal. I. Title
HG179.W527　　　　　1995
332.024—dc20　　　　　　　　　　94-45484
　　　　　　　　　　　　　　　　　　　　CIP

ISBN 1-56170-168-8

01 00 99 98　　10 9 8 7

First Published in 1989 By Nacson & Sons, Pty., Sydney, Australia
Second Printing, January 1995, by Hay House, Inc.
Seventh Printing, February 1998

Printed in the United States of America

✦ ✦ ✦

*"This book is dedicated to
the Gods of Liquidity.
May they smile favorably on
each and every one of us!"*
— Stuart Wilde

✦ ✦ ✦

Contents

✦ ✦ ✦

The Trick to Money Is Having Some!

Money is a thought-form. It is a symbol of energy, and as such, it has no real, intrinsic value. It is neither good nor bad, positive nor negative. It is impartial. The guy who wrote that "money is the root of all evil" just flat out didn't have any! You can't make it through the physical plane without it. And whereas sometimes the love of money can cause people to become evil and weird, it is a fact that without money you cannot be free. Poverty is restriction, and, as such, it is the greatest injustice you can perpetrate upon yourself.

💰 DOLLAR-DANCE CONCEPT 1 💰

*"Abundance will never be a factor of how much money one has. Rather, it is always a factor of how one **feels** about what money one **does** have."*

Yet when you look at nature and you see the abundance and flow that are naturally a part of our environment, it is hard to understand why people take up poverty as a way of life. It seems that in order to be poor, a person has to work so hard. It takes a constant effort of mind to avoid the abundance that life offers naturally. In the same way that joy is natural and God-given, so too is abundance; everything else is a drag.

If you were to carefully analyze the feelings of a tramp and a mega-millionaire, you would be amazed to find only a very slight variation in how each feels about abundance. Then if you look at the people you know and compare the successes to the failures, you will again find that the difference between them is only that of a thought-form. The successful ones often started off as failures, and then one day they changed their minds and never looked back.

What are we looking at in this book is: How are you going to change your feelings so that you make lots of money quickly, reclaim your power, and trot off into the sunset absolutely free?

By the time you reach the end of this book, I hope you will agree that the acquisition of money is not a serious business; it's a game that you play. At first it may seem that it is a game that you play with forces *outside* of yourself—the economies of the marketplace, so to speak—but as you proceed, you discover that it is actually a game you play with *yourself*. How you play that game affects the quality of your life and determines the extent to which you can liberate yourself.

To liberate yourself, you have to review what it is you believe about abundance and finances so that you can fashion an appropriate *battle plan* that will take you from struggle into flow, from skimpy into lush. Now if you have any thoughts about money not being *spiritual*, I hope that by the end of this book I will have pummeled them out of you, because that idea is absolutely ludicrous. It is a handy ego trip for all those who are too apathetic to do anything about their condition.

I believe that in life we are all on a *quest*. You may not necessarily describe your life in those terms, but I believe we are here to understand ourselves: that means physical body, intellect, emotions, spirituality, sexuality, love, motherhood, fatherhood, and cash. You have to have it—otherwise the tail wags the dog.

The whole trick to money is having some. There is really nothing else to it. That might sound a bit glib, but only to a person who doesn't have any money. If you have money, you will know that how you got it was by having it. I will explain the subtlety of this later.

Okay—onward and upwards! There are loads of ways of becoming rich. Let us eliminate some of the obvious ones so that we can concentrate on those circumstances in which most of us find ourselves.

First, you can inherit it. But if you were not born into a wealthy family, acquiring relatives who are loaded is not a simple process, although it is not impossible.

You could be adopted. You could hang out with wealthy folk and become so valuable to them and affect their feelings so dramatically that they consider you a relative even though you are not. You could marry into money. Perhaps you already have, and the fellow keeled over after a year or so, and you are sitting on a beach in Hawaii sipping Margaritas, saying, "Simple, really." Of course, you could become rich by stealing the money. That achieves the end result for you, but with it comes certain nasty implications. You would be a little disappointed to discover that, once you had filched the million you set your heart on, it did not in fact set you free. Most likely you would find yourself in the emotional trap of constantly listening for footsteps up the stairs, wondering when the heat was going to show.

Further, if you steal money, it has karmic implications, and as the money came easily to you, there will be a tendency for you to let it go the same way. Life has a balance of its own. A man I knew committed, with others, one of the most famous robberies in the history of British crime. His mates were caught and went to prison, but he remained a free man because of an incredible fluke.

The police made a clerical error early in their investigations and got his identity confused with another's. So as the case wrapped up, the police were satisfied that they had all the perpetrators under lock and key. Yet, in the confusion, my friend got away.

The pack of money he stole, however, brought him no comfort, and eventually he drifted into drugs and became a heroin addict. Whatever became of him I do not know, but when I last saw him, his condition was pitiful and his life a disaster. The problem with theft is that it is an affirmation of lack. It affirms that you do not believe that you have it in you to "play the game" and do well no matter what. The motivations of larceny are so destructive. They carry with them an implied disease that eventually shows up in the thief's life as weakness, and causes him or her misery.

In a world where there are so many crooks and chiselers, where so often people are out to make a quick buck, it is satisfying to set rules for oneself that are honorable and fair. Perhaps, by living by these rules, the point of your eventual financial freedom is delayed somewhat, but in reaching it eventually, you can look back and see that each step added to the goodness of the world, and each move allowed you to become a better human being.

The reason why making money is such a joy is that it allows you to grow spiritually, to understand the finer subtleties of life, and to come to grips with many aspects of yourself. This does not imply that rich people are necessarily spiritual, but it does infer that poor people probably are not.

Of course, if you get up and say that to an audience, a dozen people will protest and say, "What about someone like Mother Teresa?" The fact is that Mother Teresa was sold in the P.R. package as this little ol' dear who didn't have any money, but was doing good things for the Lord and the indigent of India. On one level that may have been true, and no one can argue that the folk in Bombay desperately needed her services. But if truth be known, Mother Teresa was a multimillion dollar business that was supported by the massive wealth and power of the Catholic Church. She formed a pivotal part in the merchandising of their philosophy and the solicitation of money. She was a business. She used her enthusiasm and energy to hit up the Church or the Indian government or whoever she could for cash, which she converted into resources.

Basically, she was a distributor, with a multimillion dollar budget and plenty of free labor that she was happy to use to materialize her plan. The fact that she was a good person cannot be denied, but it is also a fact that Mother Teresa was a shrewd old bird who knew how to turn a buck or two. She worked for an organization that supports a massive P.R. budget and that knows the game inside and out. Her church has more resources and a greater net worth than does General Motors. To use her as an example of poverty's being spiritual is to buy the P.R. and not the facts. Spiritual means integration with the God-force in all things, and since the God-force is abundant, it is impossible to consider oneself *truly* integrated if one does not have the same qualities as the God-force.

All philosophies that teach that poverty is groovy do so as a cop-out. It keeps the nonperforming members happy, for they can live in the ego trip of thinking that somehow their lack of creativity and effort will be blessed at a later date. I think they are in for a rude awakening, but that is irrelevant. What is important is that you agree with yourself that what you are going to contribute to the world is *energy*.

One of those forms of energy is money—money that you can give away, money with which you can empower others, money that you can use to make the world a better place, money to set you free.

Of course, money is only one form of abundance. There is also the abundance of happiness, of love, of opportunity, of friendship. But it is often true that a person who is lacking in money is also lacking in other forms of abundance. It is various aspects of their feelings that cut them off from the supply.

As was said, the difference between having money and not having it is not great. It is a very small but subtle shift in consciousness—that's all. You can see it clearly on a large scale by watching corporations that are doing fine one minute, making fifty to a hundred million a year. Then, the next day there is a small shift someplace, and they are paying more for their materials, getting less in return, and what they have is not as valuable as it was the day before. Suddenly they are losing ten million a month. Watching money at that level shows you how a small shift can make a huge difference. The name of the game is to shift yourself to the positive side and step up and collect.

Of course, people who don't have money will tell you that the world is short of the stuff. Nothing could be further from the truth. In fact, on any given working day, there are many hundreds of millions of dollars created that were not there 24 hours earlier. To get into the action, you only have to agree to play the game, the rules of which were written sometime ago. You may have to adapt to how the game is played, but once you understand that it is a game and agree to join, it is only a matter of time before the system declares you in!

Now if you do not currently see yourself as a part of great wealth, think of this: Most large financial transactions travel by satellite communications. Billions of dollars are flying through the air at close to the speed of light at any given moment. Those signals, like TV and radio signals, are constantly moving through your body. Right at this moment as you read this book, there is enough money passing through you to keep you in clover for the rest of your days. Nice affirmation? The only problem is that the money isn't yours! But that's just a minor technicality. The fact is, it is there. You are close to the goal. All it takes for it to become yours is for you and your actions to agree with that affirmation.

Of course, you could win a lottery, but most people don't believe that they can do that. However, in any lottery there has to be a winner. Deciding that that person should be you sets you ahead of the others, who, you can be sure, have agreed with themselves that their chances of winning are remote.

I know a woman in Maryland who needed a lot of money quickly. She bought *Miracles*, a little book I wrote that shows you how to lay out a miracle "action plan," and she visualized and affirmed and followed the plan. Now, this lady must have agreed with her *inner self* that it was time for her situation to change, for on the same day that she wrote out her plan, she bought $30 worth of tickets in the Maryland lottery. The lottery officials called on her a few days later to congratulate her on winning first prize. I don't remember exactly how much she won, but the figure of one million seven hundred thousand sticks in my mind. Mind you, 1.7 million sticks in anyone's mind!

I met her again a couple of months after her win and asked her how she did it. She told me that she had been affirming her abundance for some time, that the miracle action plan served as a focus of her energy and that, as she decided to buy the tickets, she agreed to win. Better still, she *knew* she had won.

Now this lady was very unusual, for most people who need money allow the emotions arising from their lack to swamp them into negative patterns that only confirm that lack. But, in spite of the fact that her situation looked desperate, she did not buy into the desperation. Instead she bought into the solution.

Interestingly enough, the other day, shortly after I started to write this book, a person whom I had met at a seminar in Colorado called me. She said that she'd had a dream in which she had dreamed the winning numbers in the Arizona lottery. The next day she drove from Colorado to Arizona to buy her tickets. On the way over, she changed her mind about the last two numbers in the dream, and instead of backing the dream numbers, she opted for three of the numbers in her dream and two others. The numbers in her dream won. Three prize winners each got $800,000. She got nothing.

I asked her why she had not invested an extra dollar in the dream numbers. She did not know. In talking to her, I genuinely felt that she could do it again, and I told her so. But also I could tell from the conversation that, although intellectually she had accepted the idea of being rich, her *inner mind* did not agree with the idea so it constantly sabotaged her efforts. Sometime in the past she must have agreed with herself that poverty would be her perpetual state, so her actions were constantly bent on ensuring that to be the fact.

Yet we are all interconnected by one energy. Jung called it the *collective unconscious*. Others might say that it is *spirit* or the grace of God, but that connection is there. All information is available to us through inner knowing. And there is hardly a person alive who has not had an ESP experience at some time or other in his or her life. Now, rather than seeing your dead granny drifting through the hallways of your house, why not agree with yourself that the next ESP experience you have should be a money-making proposition.

It's not that hard. But you'll have to get used to backing your hunches. What does it matter if you are wrong? How many times have you had a terrific intuitive feeling and then kicked yourself when you did not follow through? I have always had a great love for horse racing. The sport of kings, they call it. The problem is, it takes a king's ransom to sustain one's interest. In any race there is absolutely no logical reason why any particular horse should win. But one will. And that one horse is included in the runners and riders, so discovering it is not an impossibility.

Now, whenever you back a horse because you think it's going to win, you enter a crapshoot in which anything can happen. The problem is that you can't talk to a horse and say, "Oy mate, are you up for it today or not?" Yet every so often you'll be lounging at the paddock watching the horse parade, and suddenly you will *know* which horse is going to win. There is something about that horse's energy that has *winner* embossed on its backside. It's a wonderful feeling when that happens, for it is the only time that your money is not at risk. Plus, whenever I get one of these inner flashes, I like to hang around where the punters are placing their bets and watch their emotions flip-flop them into the wrong decisions.

Of course, the reason why most people lose is because they feel that they don't have enough money, and those emotions serve to separate them from what money they do have. The only gamblers I know who are successful are those who were well off in the first place, who were able to emotionally and financially sustain a number of losses in order to make a profit.

Of course, the other way that you can acquire lots of money quickly is to find it. Every moment of every day vast sums of money are lost. Much of that money is sooner or later found. All you have to do is set it up in your mind that you are open to finding money and that you agree to allow your intuition to place you always in the right place at the right time. Bit by bit, *money* starts to find *you*.

In the metaphysical dollar-dance of life, money is only energy. All energy is a part of the God-force, and therefore free. So in theory, money is free. What traps money is the mind and emotions of those who own it. When it drops from their possession in some way, it is liberated from their emotions, and it returns to the source. If you truly see yourself as an infinite part of all things, you *are* that source.

A man I worked with once entered a phone booth on a busy street in London. As he dialed his call and placed his money in the slot, he found that his coin was bent. Having no other coins in his pocket, he crossed the road and got some change at the paper shop. Some minutes later, when he finally returned to the booth, he found to his surprise that someone had left a suitcase there. There was no name tag on it, and my friend was in a hurry, so he just tossed the suitcase in the back of his car and continued with his day. When he got home that night, he opened the case to see if he could identify its owner. In it was a quarter of a million pounds in cash, and nothing else.

When I agreed with myself to accept all the money that the Universal Law had to offer, I went through a dramatic change in consciousness. First, I had to agree that I was worthy of receiving free money. Second, I had to know that it was okay to get money without any effort at all. By then I had gone beyond the idea that money only comes from working hard. Further, I opened myself up to receiving money by constantly picking up all the money that I found.

In the first few months of this new affirmation, I found six purses. On one occasion I was standing on the corner of a street in London. A taxi came round the curb, and a lady's handbag came flying out of the window. I hollered to the occupants, but they never heard me. I didn't make large sums at this, for if a purse had the person's I.D., I always returned it. But I did get to date some interesting ladies, all of whom were positively disposed toward me on account of my gallant chivalry...tee-hee.

What the handbag routine did for me was to help my mind exercise itself into getting ready to accept money. About a year later, $10,000 dropped into my lap. It wasn't found in the street, but it did come by a freak of chance. I bought a shipment of denim jeans in L.A. from a clothing broker, and I gave him a check in settlement. The jeans were shipped to London, and my customer wired me the $10,000 I had laid out, plus my profit.

Three months later, I noticed that the $10,000 check I gave the broker had not reached my bank. I wanted to know if he had cashed my check, and his bookkeeper confirmed that he had and showed me the deposit slip. The broker's account had been credited by his bank, but somehow the check had not reached my bank. Now, if you know anything about banking, you'll know that that's impossible. But that is exactly what happened. It could be that my check was not lost by the broker's bank, but by one of the other banks that may have been involved in processing the transaction, but the final result was that a bank somewhere laid out $10,000 on my behalf and did not instigate the paperwork to get it back. Bingo! "The Universal Law delivers $10,000 to the needy from a bank that has so much that the odd $10,000 doesn't matter." Love it! By the way, this incident was the first of many drop-in-the-lap financial gifts that I have received in the last ten years. You can do the same, even better, once you set yourself into the flow.

For the most part, *free money* will only amount to a small percentage of all the money and abundance you receive. Usually your cash flow will result from earning or working for it. Both take effort, and neither needs to involve struggle. The trick is to see your life in terms of energy. The work you do or the investments you make are a part of that overall energy. Thus, the money you receive from those efforts is also energy. By dealing with abundance in *energy* terms rather than specific dollar values, you open yourself up to receive infinite amounts, for there is no limit to energy. And as energy is abstract to the mind, it is easy for the mind to accept, whereas it is harder for the mind to accept infinite amounts of money as being a real possibility.

By following the concepts in this book, you create the metaphysics of money in the total energy of what you are—mind, body, and spirit. Then it becomes simple to develop an ESP about money, for your every fiber is attuned to the idea. To refine this, all you have to do is to convert energy into cash. This is so you can develop your battle plan for life with all of the pleasant qualities of reaching the final goal in the not-too-distant future, long before you're too old or decrepit to enjoy it.

"To the flag ye sons of freedom, to the flag."

2

Tick-Tock:
The Destiny of
the Masses

In the ordinary world of mechanical-man (*tick-tock* as I call it), money is the key symbol of survival. If I don't get some money, I don't eat; if I don't eat, I die. It is also a key symbol for the ego, for many evaluate their worth according to what possession or standard of living they enjoy. They buy things that they can show to others, so—hopefully—others will consider them important or better for having acquired whatever it is that is on display that week.

Because the ego's overriding function is to sustain the individual's survival, and because money is one of the guarantees of that survival, it is natural that the ego/personality is obsessed emotionally with finances and abundance. Yet, it is the emotions we experience around money that cut us off from easily obtaining all that we will ever need. It is the prison we create in our feelings.

Our world is abundant. There is a surplus of food, money, and resources. In fact, if the total wealth of the world were divided equally among all of its citizens, every man, woman, and child would be a millionaire. Yet we experience lack. Why? Because only a very small percentage of people are free of negative emotions around money, and even fewer have a certainty in their heart that says, "I am always in the right place at the right time, abundance is simple and natural to me, and all of my needs are constantly met."

If you were to interview people in the street, you would not find one in a hundred who would tell you that he enjoyed a surplus, an overbrimming joy in the lushness of things. Each would describe his financial limitation and insecurities by reflecting on his lack or by highlighting the lack he perceived in others. You would hear of the Ethiopians, the dole lines, the unemployed. You have to listen to stories of rising prices and economic uncertainty. You would hear the ego/personality bemoaning its lack of certainty, the absence of guarantees, the frailty of human life. Then you would understand why the world is so troubled by finances and why most never achieve a level of financial security that satisfies them.

Abundance will never be a factor of how much money one has. Rather it is always a factor of how one *feels* about what money one *does* have. And because the ego of mechanical-man is sentenced to perpetual insecurity, it follows that the proprietor of such a personality can never cross the threshold of uncertainty to a life of peace and calm. It is almost as if, in the anguish of uncertainty, erratic cash flow, and limited resources, the ego perpetuates its control over the individual by creating a constant reminder to that person of the potential disaster that is but 'round the next corner.

And having money does not necessarily alleviate the oppression of that prison, nor does it always set people free. So before we look at how you are going to make a great dollop of cash, we ought to look at what you consider freedom to be, and we should also go over one or two of the common traps of wealth. Many of the rich and famous are as miserable as sin, and their money grants them neither joy nor freedom. Further, their ego trips around wealth make them ugly, and the encumbrance of their wealth, added to the obsessive fears they have about losing it, destroys the joy that ought to be a part of their life.

Of course, it is better to be rich and miserable than poor and miserable, but neither state is completely satisfactory, and both states fuel the ego—even poverty, which is often a massive ego-trip unto itself. Of course, people who endorse poverty and believe in it as a way of life will tell you that it is not the fault of the poor that they have no money. The blame is always shifted to some outside force that is supposed to have caused the lack. They would have you believe that poverty is a disease you catch, like the clap, that the indigent are helpless victims of an economic nutcracker that has them gripped by some most delicate part of their anatomy.

For some that may be true, but for most, they are gripped only by ineptitude and apathy. I do not buy into the "disadvantaged people" excuse, for I have personally met so many who have dragged themselves up from all sorts of difficult positions and circumstances. If you have nothing, no resources, and few contacts, you are at least not encumbered by too much responsibility, and you hold to yourself the affirmation that from here, everything is up.

Often a person will consider himself to be above money and feel so godly or so intellectually superior that he doesn't need to soil his hands with day-to-day reality. Usually this type expects the world to keep him sustained, and he is often angry when the system does not recognize his specialness.

This is not a book for political discussion, but it seems to me that socialist societies breed in people a state of perpetual helplessness, because the government underwrites and guarantees the welfare of the people. Creativity loses its impetus, for it is no longer necessary as a quality in each person's survival. Thus, the system creates a class of people whose only creativity is to invent ways of milking the system. In turn, the drain of this deadweight is billed to those who, through pride or necessity, actually work.

It seems to me that when you rely on another to sustain you, you automatically have to sell your soul into slavery. The exception is perhaps a nonworking married mother, who, through her dedication to the family, accepts a certain loss of financial independence. Without income you have no freedom, and whereas it might be fun to lounge around for a little while, eventually you have to reconcile your ineptitude and subservience and tell yourself a pack of lies in order to sustain any self-worth or image. Eventually, that lack of self-worth or of self-sustaining charisma shows up in your life in various nasty little incidents of negativity that serve to confirm the uncomfortableness of things.

If you were to unplug the supposedly helpless people from the government nipple, you would be amazed to find that everyone would trot off to work the following morning like good 'uns. For whereas these people have a vested interest in sustaining a theater of hopeless circumstances, they are not necessarily into starving. The problem is that the systems that have been developed in Europe and the United States are not easily unraveled, for the people who get the handouts (and there are 38 million of them in the U.S.) are also the voters. No politician can get up on his podium and actually speak the truth. Further, there is a natural tendency for politicians to dish out money willy-nilly. First, it wins votes, and, second, it is not their money.

But in the end, these socialist societies will fall apart. For the sheer weight of this ever-expanding largesse is collapsing the economies of the world. But interestingly enough, it is not the economics of this nonsense that will bring it down—it is the metaphysics and psychology of socialism that will eventually modify the system.

Everyone who is currently coddled and sustained knows, deep within, that they are buying into metaphysical weakness borne out in their thinking by the psychology of helplessness. This eventually creates a society in which people feel that everything is hopeless and that there is no meaning to life. As this vapid and barren emotion emanates from the psyche of the people, it begins to change the outer circumstances of life. People drift into ever-deepening spirals of mind-numbing apathy, seeking whatever respite they can. Thus drugs, violence, booze, and casual sex become the only avenues of escape. As morality changes, our societies decay, and eventually there is no way to alleviate the people's discontent. The discomfort is self-perpetuating, for the life-sustaining excitement and charisma that would allow them to feel involved, to feel that they had worth, to feel they could contribute to making the world a better place, is not there.

Eventually, this lack of release turns to anger. As that anger builds, the society looks outside itself to discover something or someone on which to settle the blame. Eventually, the only way to alleviate the anger and discontent of the people is for everyone to go to war. Look at the history of Germany in the 1920s and '30s. The people and its government suffered horrendous economic collapse. It's easy to see why Hitler got off to a flying start. Or look at Iran in the modern day. When the Ayatollah Khomeini could not deliver to the people on an energy level the Islamic heaven he had promised, the only other option was to release the frustration by going to war with the neighbor, Iraq. War serves several functions. First, it acts as an enema for the discomfort and anger people feel. Second, it distracts everyone from the failures of their leaders. Third, it gets everyone involved, and finally, life takes on a new meaning as people discover their worth in the heroism of disaster. Added to that, the society and its economy is destroyed, which creates a dandy excuse for the government. Everything can begin again, somewhat bruised, but fresh and new.

Now, you may say that this cannot possibly happen, but the fact is that it is happening, and the final conclusion is but a few years away. For when you entrap the people with the fire-water of socialism, the economy comes under such strain that eventually the system destroys itself.

It is better, therefore, that you decide to become independent and self-supporting, for not only is it metaphysically correct, but in it lies the secret of true freedom. For the creative endeavors that you must employ to reach that state create around you a life-sustaining energy that will allow you respite and will pull you out of the destiny of the masses.

But, you may say, if the world is falling apart and if it's all going to the dogs in a few years' time, what, then, is the point of making money or of developing anything in particular? First of all, it may not happen if enough people change their minds. Second, the answer lies in the doing of it. Does the daffodil say it won't bother to struggle up through the ground, for it may freeze, and anyway in October its petals will wilt? Plus, it's better to be rich than poor when things fall apart. In bad times, the rich usually get richer.

As you commit to your own freedom, the level of discomfort dissipates, and bit by bit, you discover a new person, a person who has no need to alleviate his or her discomfort by taking it out on others.

Contrary to popular myth, most people survive wars. Only a very small percentage of the population is wiped out. Most Germans survived World War II, as did most of the British, French, Americans, Australians, and others involved. Those who died were souls who had metaphysically finished their current evolution on the earth plane. The rest who died were those who, not being particularly strong, or who being particularly thick when it came to reading circumstances, got sucked into the national karma and were overwhelmed by events. Now, can you see the importance of becoming independent and strong?

The idea that events happen indiscriminately and that people are just contestants in a lottery of fate is not metaphysically correct. Each drives his own destiny to whatever conclusion fits with his level of energy and the quality, or lack thereof, in his feelings. To say that the victims of the last war were innocently slain is, on an outer level, correct as many were pulled in through no apparent volition of their own. But each had an inner prompting of which we know nothing.

If you accept that you are in control of your own life and that the circumstances of that life are directed by whatever energy you put out, then you would also have to extend that concept to those alive in the 1940s. What metaphysical forces pulled those people into circumstances that ensured their departure from the physical plane, and what aspects of the same force inspired others to survive, we can never know.

But as the world changes over the next few years and the economies of the world unravel, you can be sure that people will invent all sorts of interesting forms of *hara-kiri.* Yet within that you will find others (the vast majority) who will survive, prosper, and do extremely well. The great upheavals of the world are just self-transformational seminars that a lot of very unconscious people are forced to attend so that they look at their lives under pressure.

If you don't change, reality in the end forces that change upon you. But the ego/personality hates change. If the salt-and-pepper shakers switch positions and are now at the other end of the table, "My God! What's happened?" The mind likes things steady and constantly the same. Yet if you are alive to your possibilities, you will know there is more money to be made when things are under pressure than when things are stable. For when things are steady, everyone feels secure and prices remain firm. But once the ol' stock market tumbles 500 points in a day, everyone is not so sure, and at that point you can step in and create an alternative reality for everyone by paying them a little less.

Yet if you have worked on yourself and you have developed a balance and intuition about life, there is absolutely no reason why you should have to sign up for anything gruesome. In fact, you know on an *inner* level that your destiny holds a great amount of success and enlightenment, that there is in fact no limit to what you can achieve or to the level of freedom you can attain.

Which brings me via a circuitous route to an earlier point: You have to look at what you consider to be freedom. To me, the quintessence of freedom is *feeling*, not a circumstance. If you rely on circumstance to grant you freedom, it is unlikely that you will ever achieve it. For circumstances constantly change, and the very nature of your seeking freedom in things outside of yourself creates the impossibility of that in your heart.

What freedom is to you may be slightly different from what freedom is to another, but certain aspects of freedom are common to all. To be free, you have to be fluid in your lifestyle. There must be as few encumbrances in your life as possible, and whatever encumbrances you have accepted have to be joyously taken on by you.

You will have to have money. How much money depends on what you intend to do with your life and on the various aspects of your personality. But basically, you need enough cash so that life is not a pain in the neck. At what financial level you cross the pain-in-the-neck line depends on you. To some, the PIN (pain-in-the-neck) line rests at $1,000 a week. For others, nothing less than ten grand a month will do. For a third, a million a year is a tight squeeze. The name of the game is to simplify your life to such an extent that the PIN line is reduced so that your emotions around money rest in a constant state of comfort and balance.

Speaking of the PIN, it is interesting that the number that the bank gives you to operate the cash machine on the brick wall is also called the PIN. I wondered why. I finally came to the conclusion that it was called PIN because the number is a pain-in-the-neck to remember. At my bank, if you punch in your PIN incorrectly three consecutive times, the machine presumes you're a crook and eats your card. The next day you have to attend personally and beg your card back. Anyway, it won't be long before you won't need all that nonsense. You'll have all sorts of tens of thousands swishing around, and you won't have to go through the degrading performance of begging a brick wall for $20.

Once you reach that level, what you feel about abundance and finances takes on a different hue. Because you have detached from the struggle of money and because you are no longer deeply involved in the survival mode of tick-tock, the psychic forces within you that constantly push money away, rest. In your mind, you "click" money from a symbol of survival into a symbol of freedom. Suddenly, opportunities flow, money comes effortlessly, and others, seeing your composure, come around to discover how it was that you achieved that. When they show up, bill 'em!

The point is that there is no amount of money in the world that will make you comfortable if you are not comfortable with yourself. And if your life is so piled high with stuff, whether it be attitude stuff, obligation stuff, or just stuff, there is no way you will ever be able to breathe freely.

If, from the point at which you find yourself today, you cannot walk away right now, then you are not really free. If your obligations are such that they become a major part of your emotional activity, you are not free. If you have difficulty sustaining a lifestyle or position, you have trapped yourself. It is better that you live in a one-room garret with a leaky roof, than live in a large house, the mortgage payments of which are causing your colon to turn cancerous. To be stuck in tick-tock exposes you to the destiny of the masses. It bothers me to tell you this, but when things change—and they will—if you are not free by that time, the system will eat your lunch!

That is why the trick to money is having some. For with a certain amount of cash, you can dampen down whatever debilitating emotions exist. And you know that the money you do have is an affirmation that you have created it in the past and can do it again in the future.

The rich get richer. Not only because they have surpluses

with which to invest, but because of the overriding emotional release they experience from having wealth. Even if you do not have any money to speak of, you can create for the mind the illusion that what you do have is overwhelming abundance. The mind is pretty dumb, and often it can't tell the difference between illusion and reality. You can test this. Close your eyes and imagine that you are eating a very sour lemon. Your mouth will begin to salivate in spite of the fact that there is nothing in it.

In a similar fashion, you can get your mind to agree that abundance is natural, that there will always be enough, because what you have right now is enough. Once you have talked yourself into this idea, the rest is just plain sailing.

The inner energy of the world is infinite, as is your *inner mind*. You exist on an inner level in a perpetual state. Thus, if what you see around you is "not okay," then you create in your feelings the idea that you are perpetually "not okay." Everything goes, therefore, to endorse that viewpoint. If you see the world as lousy, you take on the hue of its infinite lousiness. Conversely, if you see your life as fine and abundant, even if it is not so, and if you see the world as a happy and wonderful place to be, it becomes so. You then detach from the more severe forms of survival anxiety that the mind creates. Suddenly, you enter a personal and private heaven in which all is beauty and light.

Now, at first you will have to kid the mind that this is so. But eventually of its own accord, it selects from all the possible circumstances of life events that correspond to that energy or feeling that accentuates the joyous, liberating part of life and pulls you away from ugliness and lack.

We live in incredibly heroic times. Looking back, we will see these days as the most powerful, evolving, interesting, and spiritually rewarding times in the history of man. There is more creativity and art than ever before, more opportunity, more capital and finances, more action than ever before.

There are more people clunking around on the physical plane

than ever before, and many of them are as sick as dogs. The world has never been sicker, so if you are a healer, you can be up to your armpits in people who are conking out all over the place. If you are in finances, there is money swishing around, a billion per minute. If your interest is music, there are more orchestras, record companies, and recording studios than you can ever get around to. Whatever your interest, now is the time. It baffles me how people see lack in society when there is so much of everything. It reminds me of the guy who got locked in a bakery and died of starvation. It makes no sense.

The level of sophistication is fantastic. For example, in the olden days, if you wanted to sell some shares, your broker had to run to the floor of the exchange, find the jobber, and transact your request physically with little pieces of paper. Nowadays on the New York Stock Exchange they have the ability, with computerized trading, to transact 550,000 trades—not shares—trades, in three seconds. You are looking at a market that is so sophisticated it is open all 'round the world 24 hours a day. You can be making a royal fortune while you are snoozing with a loved one—or two. Any time of the day or night, you can sit bolt upright and holler, "Sell zinc!" and someone somewhere will sell it for you. It might have to be in Kuala Lumpur because it's so late at night, but you can get out of zinc in ten seconds anytime.

Inside mass consciousness where most people live, money is a form of the God-force, the emotion of which is stronger than any religion or spiritual idea and often stronger than love or family ties. The overwhelming influence of the emotion of money dominates the people. That is why everyone is tearing around like chickens with their heads cut off, trying to get "in the money." It isn't usually the money itself that motivates tick-tock; it is the addiction of constantly having to appease the Gods of Survival.

You can probably see this, in the past, in your own life. You got emotionally involved in a financial deal or you got strung out waiting for a check to arrive in the mail, and it burned you out emotionally. When the deal finally went through or when the check plopped on your mat, you had little pleasure in it. And you transferred your emotions to the next deal and the next postal delivery.

Tick-tock deals with the surface of the physical plane only, and that is why it is hard to exist solely within it. For whereas the surface may have a lot of good ideas and methods, it is not complete without a metaphysical approach as well. Think of this: If you have done fairly well in the normal rhythm of things, two or three metaphysical ideas added to all that you already know may be all that you need to put you on top of the heap.

It's interesting to me how many of the traditional ways have changed to incorporate a mysticism and a more infinite overview. This is especially so in the big corporations where millions are being spent on motivation, consciousness raising, and leadership skills. People are catching on. All the logic and the technical approach is fine, but that is open to anyone who can pay for the software. A little metaphysics gives you a head start over the others, and it simplifies your life.

The thing about tick-tock is that the people in it believe that what they see as reality is real. That's funny—ludicrously funny. They think that life is serious, and they look at all those little pieces of green paper (or whatever color the government is using this year to pretty up the paper and make it look like it might be worth something), and they are prepared to die of cancer to get a pile of it.

Now, as you look at the way tick-tock deals with the emotion of money, all you have to do is get a little crafty and step back just one pace away from tick-tock and let them all run around like crazies. The trick is to get out of most of the emotion, to resonate a strong, steady energy and allow the natural forces of life to bring you all that you want.

An old bull and a young bull were standing on a hill overlooking a field full of very attractive cows. The young bull said to the old bull, "Let's run down there and hopefully we can grab a couple of those cows and make love to them." And the old bull, turning to the younger one and smiling, said, "No, let us walk down and we'll make love to them all."

Walk slowly with a steady pace, care for nothing much, watch what is at your feet, project little into the future, and suddenly you begin to live. You don't need a million dollars necessarily or a pile of Swiss francs in a hole in order to feel okay. It helps, but it's not vital. All you need right now is enough to get you through the next 72 hours. You don't need to ask, "How will I survive when I get to 99?" The Universal Law of abundance will say to you, "You're bananas. You're only 18; what are you worried about?"

💰 DOLLAR-DANCE CONCEPT 2 💰

"Even if you do not have any money to speak of, you can create for the mind the illusion that what you do have is overwhelming abundance."

If you have made it in life up to this point, why would you not make it farther down the line? Surely you are becoming more aware, more conscious, more crafty, developing a stronger and stronger sense of your own identity. If you stay balanced and develop a calm around finances, you are bound to have all the money you will ever need. There may be harvest, and other times will be for planting and may be more sparse, but that is natural. You can agree right now that you will never have to put out another thought about money ever again. For it is not real, it is not scarce, it is not negative. It's just little pieces of colored paper—a complete nonsense, but tick-tock believes in it. In reality, there is no limit to how many of those bits of paper you can have; all you have to do is to get in the flow and agree with your *inner self* that the idea is compatible.

3

Pulling People Through Acceptance

The ego seeks approval. People seek approval. We all come through an educational training where we teach our kids to do little things, and we pat them on the head and give them a chocolate. "Did I do okay, Mummy?" "Sure, you did okay," Pat pat.

The family is where the ego learns to look for approval, and then, as the person grows up, he or she goes out into the world to win the approval of everyone else. The ego is influenced by everything everyone else wants. Why? 'Coz it's stupid. Why would it fall for a stunt like that? But it does, constantly.

"We want you to do this and that, otherwise we won't love you. We want you to do the dishes."

"You mean I have to?"

"Yes. We want you to wash these dishes."

"What, today?"

"No. Every day."

"Well, just one dish?"

"No. Two hundred and ninety-one of them, every day."

"What, for a week?"

"No, for the rest of your life!"

"That's what I have to do in order for you to love me?"

"Yes. Once you prove to us that you are that stupid, we'll agree to love you."

The male version goes like this: "We want you to bolt out the door at ten-till-dawn, belt up and down the freeway, pressurize yourself totally stupid for 19 hours a day with all sorts of concepts about working hard, and drag home enough buffalo, or cash, or moola, so we here will feel safe. Then if we feel safe and secure because of the sheer amount of buffalo you haul home, then we'll love you."

So the male ego goes, "Oh, all right." And off he trudges and dies! And they say, "Harry died on the freeway, aged 42—three buffalo on the backseat."

The point is that we are constantly trying to win people's approval because we are not taught to grant ourselves our own approval. In doing so, we usually spend a lot of cash frantically buying things and giving money away, hoping that somehow these actions will make us okay. I noticed that in Australia the average male is very wrapped up with the idea that people should consider him a "good bloke." In trying to win people's approval, he gives away some of his power, and it exposes him to being manipulated.

Either people accept you or they don't. You did not come here to be manipulated, just to keep people happy. What you are is what you are. You can change it. But first you have to accept it, for it is the truth. In accepting yourself, you don't have to get into a huge ego trip, but you do have to come to the point of being satisfied with what you are.

None of us is perfect, otherwise we would not be here. The very virtue of the quest is that much of it lies ahead. But as long as you are making progress, you can settle into the fact that you don't have it all together. You can be happy that sometimes you arrive late, or that occasionally you have let people down, or that your checks bounce, or whatever.

Yet, we tend to let ourselves get sucked into other people's opinions, and we buy into what they think we should be. So the next time you bounce the rent check on the landlord, instead of feeling rotten and listening to all the things he or she might have to say about your flakiness, just smile sweetly, shrug, and say, "Aerobic checks. They bounce around a lot." You are eternal, immortal, and infinite. The fact that you can't count is just a minor aberration.

Once you can accept yourself and feel comfortable with that, then the world accepts you. And when your checks bounce, they'll make excuses for you, saying it probably wasn't your fault. It is only when you feel insecure about who you are that other people don't like you. Have you ever wondered why? Because basically, people who don't accept themselves are very insecure. That insecurity is projected, and others react negatively. It reminds them of their own vulnerability.

You can see this clearly in people who play "victim." They put out a constant "poor me" energy, hoping to win people's affection by twanging their emotions. Yet "victim" as a theatrical role doesn't work, for while someone is telling you this week's crop of horror stories, you often find yourself becoming more and more angry. You feel like smacking them in the mouth saying, "Here, let me help you. Let me jump on your head. Let me slap you in the eye with this wet haddock—now, how do you feel? Happy, are you? It's only 9:15. I could probably arrange another assault about lunchtime; that any good to you?"

In order for you to become wealthy, you are going to have to become good at accepting things—very good. By accepting yourself, that becomes easier. Of course there are loads of very rich people who do not accept themselves for one minute, but what is the point of having money and not having a settled life? I have never seen the reason for all the guilt trips and inadequacies that people go through. I can see why they go through it and how it came about, but I feel that they ought to give themselves an even break. It is not that hard to back off.

Buying into what everyone else says you should do disempowers you. It serves as a constant reminder that you are not in control of your life. It's better, therefore, that you go out into the world, live on your own away from social pressure, and make loads of silly mistakes, than that you live in a close-knit community in which you allow yourself to be trapped by the attitudes of all the people around you.

It may be that the advice you receive is good advice, but it is important that you make that advice yours. It has to be what you want, and it has to come from your ideas and lifestyle, not from the motivations of others. Once you get centered and discover who you are, and are happy with that, you begin to pull out of the general destiny of the world. You become a true individual, driving your own metaphysical bus, so to speak. That is vitally important, for the world of tick-tock is heading for a brick wall, and if you just follow along like a moron, you rest inside the collective destiny rather than inside a fresher, more liberating destiny of your own. It allows you to instigate change in your life without the interference of others. It is you, freeing yourself up to change yourself.

What usually occurs is that the ego/personality resists change. Then it has no emotional fortitude for that change when it eventually happens. Often the ego/personality will have such a vested emotional interest in the *status quo* that it feels that the status quo *is* itself. Then if reality changes, or collapses, its life collapses with it. So you see stockbrokers swallow-diving off highrises when the market falls.

In the dollar-dance of life, acceptance is a key issue for most. It is the block that holds so many back. Its psychic undercurrent slows their progress to a crawl. Once you can accept yourself, then you can begin to look at the level of acceptance you offer to others. The subtlety here is not to create an abrasive attitude toward the actions of others, even if you do not agree. For, as you put out negative aggression, it ruins your own fluidity and flow. You can't spend 20 minutes raving on about how rotten your neighbor is without that criticism becoming a part of your own reality. The *inner you*, existing as it does as a part of all things, has difficulty differentiating between you and your neighbor. It has a tendency to believe that what you're saying about another is in fact what you believe about yourself.

💰 DOLLAR-DANCE CONCEPT 3 💰

"Acceptance (of self) is the foundation of receiving."

So in the same way that you ought to give yourself an even break, you should offer those around you an even better deal, for they may not have the advantage of being a living genius like you. Further, it's a training in self-acceptance to allow everyone to be as silly as they want for as long as they want. Soon you become more tolerant of your own shortcomings.

Acceptance is the foundation of receiving. It is also the way that you pull people to you, for when you can accept yourself and others, a calm exists all around you. That energy exudes an unusual power. People are fascinated by it. They feel secure within it and are automatically drawn to it. By being liberal with others, you liberate yourself.

Then, in order for you to crank up your level of financial activity, you will have to open to receiving, and you will have to ensure that there is no part of your intellect or of your *inner self* that is against it.

The guy who wrote that it is more blessed to give than to receive was the fellow who was getting it! In the eternal inner reality, there is no difference—neither is higher nor lower. Both giving and receiving is energy in flow, but it is all a part of the same energy. What one has done is just to shift it somewhere. Imagine it like this: If you took a million gallons of water out of the ocean off the coast of California and took it north and dropped it back into the ocean off the coast of Seattle, it wouldn't make any difference to the total or to the quality or the nature of all the water in the Pacific Ocean.

Even if you dropped the million gallons on Seattle itself, it wouldn't make a lot of difference. The citizens there are used to it! It is the only place in the world where the clouds hover at zero altitude, and rain falls from the ground up!

The point is that if you accept that there is only one energy in all things, then on an energy level there is no giving or receiving— just energy moving around within itself. It's only the ego that sees a separateness in things. So the ego will say, "The Cadillac went from Harry to Sally." But on an infinite level, it is neither Harry's nor Sally's, it is a part of all things. It *is*. Where it finds itself and whose name is on the owner's manual is irrelevant.

This means that in the infinity of things, all the money in the world is, in effect, yours. At least you can begin to feel that it is. You can open to the idea that it is natural for people to give you money and things. You can invent exercises that help you to understand receiving. By the end of this book, I want you to be so good at receiving that we'd nominate you for the "Receiving Oscar" of life.

It takes practice. But you can start by never turning anything down. Accept everything you are offered by others even if you have no need for the object. Take it. You can always toss it out later or give it to someone else who is in the "receiving" training. That's important. And as you accept a gift or favor or money, watch how you react. See if you can take that thing graciously and naturally, or if you react with emotional embarrassment. See if your reaction is an open or closed one.

So the next time one of your mates offers you a psychedelic fluorescent tie with a nude on it that moves when you move, rather than thinking, *Shall I throw up now or later?* accept it. Realize that it isn't the tie that is important; it is your ability to take things as they come along. It is your affirmation that you are worthy of gifts, that you are open to receive.

But you have to be consistent so that the various parts of yourself are not tugging in opposite directions. Agree to accept all the money that comes your way. That means that you can't see a penny on the sidewalk and walk past it. You will have to be consistent in your affirmation, and pick up each and every penny you find—even the horrible ones that are stuck to the pavement with chewing gum. The reason for this is that the collective unconscious, or Universal Law, as I like to call it, is not aware of value. If you affirm, "I am abundant; money comes to me," and then see a penny in the street and can't be bothered to pick it up, the message you put out by your action is not in sync with your affirmation; thus, you disempower your abundance consciousness.

Now, sometimes picking up a penny, especially when you are with other people, can be embarrassing, for they don't do things like that. They're much too important to accept something for nothing. But the fact that it is embarrassing is excellent training, for you have to go past that idea and act for yourself, not in accordance with what others might think.

Some years ago in London, I was entertaining a group of very important business folk from the U.S. I had decided to take them to the ballet at the Royal Opera House, Covent Garden. I thought that this would be a nice, swanky way of showing them the top-of-the-line. Now in those days, I had been banned from driving for having too much blood in my alcohol stream. So I had bought a Rolls and hired a chauffeur to get around the transport problem.

I had arranged for the driver, Slick Vic, we called him, to

wait at the curb directly outside the Opera House so that at the end of the performance I could whisk my guests off to a late-night dinner. A table for five had been reserved at the Trattoria Cost-a-Lotto.

Well, as we came out of the Opera House, crowds milling, guests in tow, I began to cross the sidewalk to the car. There to my left was a penny. It had been raining that evening, so the penny shone, reflecting the streetlights and the shadows of those lights, flickering as they did through the crowd, giving the momentary impression that the coin was, in fact, winking, taunting me to walk past it. I hesitated, wondering what everyone would think as I groped around at their feet. Then I decided that an affirmation is an affirmation, so I went for the penny.

The problem was that I was a little halfhearted, and instead of just bending down and picking the damn thing up, I did a kind of bunny dip, which entails keeping your back straight, bending your knees, and dropping your hand slightly behind you. The maneuver was taught to waitresses at the Playboy Club as a way of setting drinks on a table without having customers look down their cleavage. I can't remember who taught it to me—deep in the back of my mind there is a faint fond memory—but something must have been lost in the passage of time, for on that night I got it all wrong.

What should have been a graceful scoop turned into a fiasco. I hit the penny with my knuckles, and it began a long, loping run across the sidewalk, snaking gracefully in and around many an expensive shoe. At that point, I should have left well enough alone. But determined as I was, I refused to give up. I lunged at the itinerant coin and missed, winding up on all fours.

That night I had chosen to wear a white satin suit, God knows why. But by the time I finally had the penny in hand, I had acquired most of the muddy water on that particular sidewalk. Meanwhile, Slick Vic had ushered my guests into the car, and they relaxed to watch my pantomime with restrained astonishment.

I was really embarrassed. And once in the car, I felt I had to offer an explanation. So I told my American friends that the penny routine was an ancient British custom that brought untold amounts of good fortune. They were fascinated to learn the ins and outs of the British culture, and one of them even began taking a few notes.

All was well until he started to pin me down as to exactly how the "penny in the gutter" routine entered British folklore. At that point, I went completely over the top. I told them it was a custom handed down from Elizabethan times. To make it real, I created a whole fantastic scenario with Elizabeth and Lord Dudley. I even slung in Walter Raleigh out of politeness, thinking that perhaps my guests were none too familiar with Dudley's exploits. It wasn't long before I had Queen Elizabeth, Lord Dudley, and Walter Raleigh crawling across the floor of Hampton Court in chase of the Royal Penny.

Everyone was duly impressed with my knowledge of the more obscure parts of English history, as was I myself. I somehow felt that I had created a historic moment returning the "penny in the gutter" to its rightful place among the glories of the English-speaking people. You can just see it:

1558: Elizabeth ascends to the throne of England.
1559: The "Penny in the Gutter" enters English history.

Notes taken, events chronicled, the conversation drifted to silence. As the Rolls glided silently through the night, taking us to our rendezvous with fettuccine, linguine, and Chianti Classico, I thought about the events of the evening. I must say that secretly, I felt proud of myself, damn proud. From time to time, I surreptitiously opened my hand to glimpse the great but muddy prize, while I mused that there is no limit to abundance when you are committed to going for it.

The reason why training yourself to receive is such a spiritual experience is that it forces you to open yourself up and allows you to see that there is in fact a limitlessness to all things. Think of it like this: If you are prepared to open up, you will gradually express more and more energy, and as you express more energy, your gift to the world becomes greater. For as you give of yourself, you offer the world courage, inspiration, and a joyously happy outlook. As that energy goes from you and is allowed to mix with whatever the circumstances of the people gathered around you are, things naturally improve. It follows, then, that as a representative of the light, you would be entitled to get an equal, if not greater, amount of energy back. To those who have, more is added.

Now, that energy coming back to you might be in the form of love, opportunity, and/or just the good feelings that people have toward you. But some of that energy will be hard cash. And that's neat. However, you have to be able to graciously accept all that is coming to you, never limiting what you are prepared to receive.

In tick-tock we tend to quantify things by what they are worth. This is a natural by-product of the logical mind. So we say, "This plumbing job is worth $200." But as you start to see yourself and your actions as energy, and as that energy has worth (meaning an expansive, positive, limitless quality), there is no reason why you can't have someone pay you $5,000 to fix their leak.

Now this may seem to you unlikely. But if it does, it just means that you are still somewhat programmed into structural thinking. It is only a matter of breaking you out and allowing you to see greater possibilities.

When I first started work in 1964, I got a job as a gofer/mail boy with a firm of ship brokers in London. My gross pay was £10 per week ($17 at today's exchange rates). From that I had to deduct £1.75 tax, £1.50 for travel, £1.50 for food, and one pound a week to have my business suit dry-cleaned. My take-home pay was £4.25 a week for 40 hours.

At that time, British rock 'n' roll stars earned around $1,000 per night. That was the equivalent of two years' pay to me, and I remember thinking what an untold fortune it was. I considered singing lessons. The problem was that (1) I am tone deaf, and (2) I sound like a frog in a bag. But my lack of singing abilities was not what held me back from the magical thousand-a-night league. My problem was that I could not, at that young age, feel that I had energy to offer for which anyone would pay substantially. My mind-set was limited to £4.25 a week or thereabouts. I needed time to mature and to grow in my thinking.

Since my job was in the heart of the financial district of London, I got caught up in the *feel* of commercial activity. On my lunch hour, I would stand outside the Bank of England or the Stock Exchange and watch all the important folk coming and going. I followed the stock market day by day even though there was no way I could ever afford to buy even a single share. What I did was, I *joined* in my feelings even though my current reality was far from that world.

It wasn't long before I realized that business—not singing— was the place for me. I left my job in the city, and in less than a thousand days, I had formed my own business and was generating about $20,000 a week. I began to meet many of the more famous British pop stars, and I remember wondering how the poor devils got 'round on just a grand a night. I was still a couple of months short of my 21st birthday.

But it wasn't all plain sailing from there. It took almost 15 years for my mind to accept abundance as natural. I had times of fantastic success in which I wallowed in "lush and flush," and there were other times when I experienced excruciating difficulty and tremendous financial troubles. But in the bad times, I always kept my mind on the dream, and even though I was often being chased by a band of irate creditors, I always held a positive outlook.

I'll never forget the morning the man for the courts came 'round. I had been out with my mates, lurking and cavorting 'til dawn. An hour later, the doorbell rang. Dazed, I staggered to the door and opened it. There was an official-looking bloke with a bunch of documents in his hand. In those days, court writs were wrapped with red string, and it was the glimpse of that very same string that put me instantly on my guard.

"Mr. Wilde," said the bailiff, in a sonorous tone. But before he could utter another word, which no doubt would have contained a litany of complaints and details of who was suing me for what, I interrupted. "That bastard!" I said. "He's run away owing me three months' rent, the electricity hasn't been paid, and there are £300 of long-distance calls on the phone bill."

The man from the courts began to commiserate with me, saying how irresponsible people had become nowadays. I eventually invited him in for a cup of tea. We chatted for a while about the ins and outs of the British legal system, and the bailiff told me that serving complaints on people was not a well-paid job. "Well," I said, "if you find that bastard Wilde, I'll give you 50 pounds if you tell me where he is."

The bailiff was delighted with the possibility of some financial advancement, and he promised due diligence in his search. I saw him to the door, and slipping an extra chocolate biscuit in his pocket, I wished him all the luck in the world. Meanwhile, my mates who earlier had passed out in various locations throughout the apartment, began to congregate in the kitchen. I told them the story of the bailiff, and we all fell about laughing. Somehow, even in the negativity of learning about abundance, there was never a dull moment.

The point is that it takes time to crank your thinking up to where it will accept greater possibilities, and it is important for you not to focus on any negative setbacks. It is so easy to have one's confidence shattered by early reverses, and often those reverses become more real than they ought to be. The name of the game is to see your defeats as seminars you paid to attend to learn the game of life. It's heartening to note that many millionaires have gone bankrupt at least once or twice before they hit the jack-pot. The fact that you have the courage to step out and commit to the campaign means that from time to time you are bound to suffer setbacks. That is just the way things are. It will come right in the end. You have to have a lot of patience and tenacity to hold on while the Universal Law delivers.

It is like planting seeds. If you come back a week later, you would get the impression that nothing was happening. But you have to allow the energy to build and grow, and, as it is an esoteric energy, you will not necessarily have any outer evidence that it is working. Learn to trust, and keep your emotions out of it. Meanwhile, work on altering your mind-set to accept more.

And When They Show Up, Bill 'Em!

To "bill 'em," you will have to learn to charge people for what it is that you do or for whatever product you might supply them. Part of the dollar-dance of life is going beyond the ego's emotional awkwardness about charging money. Somehow we tend to think that when we bill someone they will not like us, or perhaps we are taking food from the mouths of babes.

This harks back to our approval complexes, but it also has a lot to do with self-confidence. One of the things you will have to look at is how you will concentrate and consolidate your energy so that you feel good about charging.

How many times have you done an incredibly neat job for someone, really put your heart and soul into it? Normally you would have charged, say, $100, but when asked how much was owed, you responded, "No, no, have it for nothing." Or you've said, "Well, I normally charge a hundred, but on this occasion I'll take ten."

We have all done it at some time or other. And, whereas it is pleasurable and kind to do someone a favor, it is also important that the level of your commercial activity endorse you, and this comes from your charging a decent price. Otherwise, the energy you expend in just making ends meet robs you of your positivity. Eventually, that lack of positivity will pull you down, and you will find that you don't even have the discount customers anymore.

Many find it hard to charge for what they do, for the ego hesitates, feeling that people will react negatively. In fact, quite the reverse is the case. People like you to charge them more. It makes them feel more important. How much buzz do you get out of spending nine cents in Woolworth's? But a $200 meal makes you feel special. You feel you are getting value. Further, the more you charge, the more people respect you. If you do things on the cheap, people tend to get down on you and find fault with what you do. Having gotten something for nothing, they begin to demand more. That's human nature.

The other thing about charging is that often we tend to think that the world is experiencing the same lack that we are. This is a bad mistake. The fact that you might be potless does not mean the world is—you should not project your lack onto others. I notice this particularly in Australia. If you go into a grocery store and buy the top-of-the-line item, the storekeeper tries to dissuade you from having it, or at very least, he warns you that you have picked the pricey item. It is as though he thinks you are going to electrocute yourself if you touch that particular can or brand of tea.

Recently in Sydney I was discussing this feature of the Australian psyche with a friend who told me that Twinings was considered the best tea and was much more expensive than other brands. So the next time I was in a store, I picked up a couple of packs of the tea and placed them on the checkout counter. Sure enough, the owner of the store said, "This is Twinings tea, ya know. It's very expensive. It costs a dollar more." I answered, "Fantastic." "No," he said, thinking that I had misheard him, "not a dollar less, a dollar more." "Great!" I exclaimed. By now the storekeeper was really confused. He had figured out that I was foreign, at least not Australian. So he started repeating himself, talking loudly and slowly as if I were a deaf Eskimo who couldn't speak English. Picking up the tea, he held the boxes to his chest and pointed to the price tag. He gripped them as if they were priceless heirlooms handed down from time immemorial. I leaned over and peered at the offending price tag and said, "I understand now."

The storekeeper beamed a smile of delight, happy that he had saved me from the grisly fate of paying a dollar more. But while he was still clutching the boxes to his chest, I turned around and lazily scanned the shelves of the shop. Then, turning ever so slowly back to face the owner, I smiled and said, "I'll take 60 boxes." He didn't believe me. So I wound up taking just the two I had originally selected, and I trotted off to ponder the ups and downs of the world tea market.

Again, you can see that the inability to charge properly comes from the common emotional conflicts people have about money. Many feel that if they charge for a service or item they are somehow taking something away from the buyer; that in their charging, the buyer's safety or survival is threatened in some way. This is pure tick-tock. You have to grant the buyer a mind of his own. He knows what he wants, and if he wants it, he'll buy it. If he doesn't want it, he usually won't.

The other emotion about charging is fear. We tend to feel that if we charge a goodly amount, somehow our market will disappear and we'll all be bankrupt next Thursday. Yet even with all the economies bouncing up and down and all the uncertainty people feel around lack, the quality items of the world go on forever. There will always be a market for Rolls Royces, French champagne, five-star hotels, and villas on the beach. All you have to do is agree to come from quality. That means energy. I'll devote a section on that, as it seems to me to be so vital.

In tick-tock, people see the marketplace with all its structures and price formats, and they feel constrained by that. They see the elements of competition, and they feel that their financial future is uncertain, which in many cases it is. But this is because, though tick-tock has products and services, for the most part it has little energy. Every hamburger joint is exactly like all the rest, as are all gas stations, Laundromats, airlines, or whatever. In a market where things are imbued with no real energy, all they can sell you is the hardcore product, which is often dissatisfying, for you feel intuitively that it has no life. It is usually flat and boring and churned out by the millions.

Once you can infuse your life's energy with enthusiasm, creativity, and originality, the things you offer the world take on a different tone. Now you are no longer competing with tick-tock, and you can charge what you like.

Remember that the spiritual energy of the earth, the God-force—put it in whatever terms you like—is not aware of worth. I know it is common for people to think of God as a fellow sitting on a throne somewhere watching everything, eyeing the price of Hondas this year. But that is not so. If you understand the metaphysical truth of the world, you will see God more as an energy than as a person. So what a Christian might see as the grace of God, an Asian would say was the eternal Tao flowing through all things. The point here is that price is only a factor of emotion, and the God-force is not involved in human emotion. In other words, the God-force has no emotional attachment to owning a new digital-diddly that opens the cat flap in the front door, say. So $10 or $60 million feels the same to it.

Worth is only a factor of emotion, nothing else. Things that people feel good about, that they want, are worth more than things they don't want. It seems to me that the God-force and the Life-force are one and the same. Your Life-force is your energy, your enthusiasm, what you put out. So if the energy that sustains the world has no idea of worth, then there is no limit to how much of that Life-force's spiritual energy you can transform into cash, should you so desire.

First, you have to liberate your feelings from any awkward-

ness about setting your prices. You just see yourself as a trans-
feror of energy. People can get things anywhere; energy is much
more rare. When you see yourself transferring energy, there is no
particular value to that energy, so there is no limit to what people
can give you, meaning that in your dedication to energy you are
in fact serving people. Not only do the things you do have a special worth, but also you allow others to discover in whatever you
do a higher ideal, an exhilaration, a *quickening*, that is not found
in the run-of-the-mill.

People have needs, and when you meet those needs you serve
them—not only because you save them the hassle of looking elsewhere—but also because what you offer has a unique specialness.
I know a guy who has a small shop that repairs electrical equip-
ment. He is a genius in his field. His energy is mature. He is like
a wise old sage. He is always packed with work, and he loves the
job he does. People come to him just to experience being with
him. They bring him things to fix. He fixes them, and a week later
they bring him the same item in perfect working order, and he
fixes it again. I asked him what his secret is. And he told me that
the items people brought to him were only symbols of their own
lives, and as he patches up their toaster, he sees himself healing
their lives as well. The customers linger in his shop, and he might
offer a word of encouragement or a positive affirmation. He
always shows them what quality is, and bit by bit, his regulars
learn about themselves and see their lives in a different light.

So once you can see that, you can relax about what price you
are charging and just work on giving people as much energy as
possible and feeling good about yourself. When people come to
you for, say, a healing massage, you say, "$100," and they say,
"Well, wasn't it only $50 last week?" You reply, "Yes, but this
week I feel good about myself. $100!"

Try this as practice: For the next 30 days, don't do anything
for anyone without charging. Force yourself to charge for everything. When you are asked to give someone a lift to the station, tell

him it will cost $20. This exercise is hard because people expect you to do all sorts of things for nothing. When you tell them it will cost them, they react. The lesson you have to learn is not to react. Also, be careful that you don't find yourself making excuses. "I have to charge you $20 because I am poor and miserable, and I am not going to survive today without your money." Just say, "You want to go to the station, fine. $20." Stand your ground. It is irrelevant if they hire you or not. The lesson lies in your becoming comfortable with telling people that you feel worthy.

In the metaphysical circles that I come from, it's called WAM, which stands for *what about me!* It is easy, isn't it, to forget to include yourself? We spend so much time helping others through a sense of dedication that we drop out on collecting a bit for ourselves. There seems to be a constant conflict between commercial activity and goodness.

The way to reconcile this is to separate the two. You can be generous and warmhearted in your personal life, but business is business. You should never forget that. In your commercial activity, you should come from an energy that demands everything. I know that nowadays the win/win method is touted as a fair solution, meaning that you get most of what you want, and the others in the negotiation get most of what they want. Everyone wins, in theory anyway.

The problem with that idea is that you go into a business meeting having given a great chunk of the high ground away in your *feeling* before you even open your mouth. It is right that things should be fair, but it is also right for you to start the conversation by demanding everything.

If you go into a deal saying, "I'll take 50 percent," your opponent can beat you down from there, and you might end up with less than half. It's better, therefore, that you operate out of WAM. Start on top of the hill. When asked how much you want, look them straight in the eye and say, "All of it." They are not going to believe what they are hearing. That's okay. You're not here to keep them happy.

Now, if your feelings are aligned to WAM, you will be comfortable in demanding 100 percent of the deal. And if they are happy with win/win, they are going to ask for 50 percent. That leaves you in the strong position of saying, "Look, I'll take 25 percent less than what I want, and you in turn take 25 percent less than you want. That's fair, isn't it?" You walk out of the door with 75 rubles to their 25.

"Fair" is anything that two or more people agree to. Now it's not my way to go out and screw people to the floor for every last dime. The effort is not worth it; everyone's entitled to turn a buck or two. But when you're presenting yourself in the marketplace, if you don't come from a position of demanding everything at the front end, you usually wind up with less than what you're worth at the back end.

How many readers of this book are doing a job today and are getting paid diddly-squat, only because seven years ago when they originally went for the job interview they were a bit nervous and forgot to *feel* worthy, so they failed to demand everything? It's only a matter of self-confidence, really.

Try saying it to yourself over and over as an affirmation. It makes you feel marvelous. "How much do you want?" "All of it!" "How much do you want?" "All of it!" "How much do you want..." Of course, it is very unusual for people to agree to give you all of it. They'll beat you down. But at least with my method, you capture all of the territory up front in your feelings, so then you have plenty to give away.

💰 DOLLAR-DANCE CONCEPT 4 💰

"Learning to charge properly is a vital key to abundance. Affirm that you will never devalue yourself by charging less than what you feel you are worth."

Of course, even in business you'll cut people some slack from time to time. But if you overdo it, you disempower yourself. In the end, your lack of financial dexterity will make you angry. You need money to fuel your quest. You have to learn to demand what you want from life, remembering that no one knows what the hell you do want till you tell them. You have to accept what's coming to you and bill people properly.

Once you are completely comfortable with charging, then—and only then—will you allow yourself to do things for free. That way if you perform a kindness for another, you will know that you are doing it because you want to, not because you have been manipulated into it or are maneuvering in the hopes of winning their affection.

The final point about charging is its great benefit to you. If you are offering a service or product, it is no fun if, in performing that service, your life becomes a negative uphill struggle. By charging a goodly amount for what you do and by coming from quality and excellence, you will naturally, without offending anyone, get rid of the lower end of the market.

As was said, only the restricted people of the world believe that there is not enough, believe in the "penny off" discount philosophy. It's hard to try to make it financially, working in that kind of market. Further, poor people are usually extremely negative and have a tendency to bring you down by constantly focusing on what *isn't* rather than on what *is*. By charging and doing things well, you automatically move up a notch or two and appeal to people who have bundles. I don't mean mega-millionaires, necessarily, but the more affluent upwardly mobile types. It is a fact that there are all sorts of people (millions of them) for whom price is irrelevant. What they want is *energy*.

That energy can be offered in beauty, service, efficiency, positivity, or value. These upwardly mobile people are usually very busy. They want things quickly and efficiently, and they want the product or service to work. What it costs is not a major factor in their decisions.

So when you invest your energy in things and they become wonderful, there is no defined limit as to what you can charge. I don't mean that you should stiff people and overcharge. What I mean is that at the lower end of the market, everyone knows exactly how many cents a carrot costs. At the upper end, the kind of people who buy endive imported from Belgium could give a damn. They just want the endive. They couldn't tell you what endive costs if their life depended on it. That is the kind of character you want to be hanging out with, because that is the kind of affluent character you want to become.

In a world where everything is so ordinary and dull and things are churned out the same way, year in and year out, if you come from a place of originality and invest energy in things, people respond. It is joy, is it not, to discover things that are special? Shops that are truly different, restaurants that actually give good service or create original food, places where people make just that little bit of extra effort—when you find such a place, you are happy to pay, for you know that the quality and fun you get is worth a hundred times the junk offered in the ordinary world.

It's not hard to be original. You have only to think in terms of what people want. Take hotels: People go there to wash up, sleep, and head out again. But the owners of those hotels spend the least amount of money in the bedrooms. Instead, they spend untold millions building the lobby. It's great for the owner's ego, but who sleeps in the lobby, for goodness' sake? Isn't it a fact that often on checking out, you feel disappointed, you feel that the hotel didn't quite come up to what you were expecting?

The other thing you want in a hotel is real service. You have to go to Europe or the East for that. It is not a part of the American psyche to serve—they find no joy in it. Even in the very best hotels in America, the service sucks. Why? Because they don't train their staff to serve. The whole system is designed to suit the convenience of the management, not the customer. Containing the service is how they trim costs.

On occasions, I have had the misfortune of being booked into one of the Marriott Hotels in the U.S. There's one at the airport in Washington, D.C. In the entrance there is a photo of ol' man Marriott himself, grinning at the suckers who are checking into his hotel. Behind the desk there's a huge sign that says something like, "We're dedicated to your service."

I had rented one of their ballrooms for a seminar. The seminar was scheduled till six in the evening, so I asked the girl at the desk if I could leave two trunks in my room, as she had already told me she was not going to be needing that room until the next day. She refused. I pointed out that I was spending untold thousands at their establishment. She still refused. I mentioned that I had pulled 250 people into their hotel, all of whom were eating lunch in their restaurant. That didn't work either. I asked her if the sign behind the desk meant anything, or was it just hiding a hole in the wall? She offered me a snotty grunt and wandered into the back room. That grunt has cost ol' man Marriott $20,000 to $30,000 so far. I have never spent another penny with that company, and none of my staff members stay there either.

Now if you and I were opening a hotel, we'd concentrate on the stuff people really want. We wouldn't mess with a stupid sign at the desk. We would give the customers the real thing. We'd spend most of our money on the rooms. The lobby would be simple and cozy, but the rooms would be lush. Have you ever noticed how rinky-dink hotel towels are? There are never enough of them. I'd get special towels made, six feet long by three feet wide. I'd give each room eight, ten, as many as they wanted. I'd build a little closet for the towels and heat them. Also, I'd give people monogrammed bathrobes with the hotel's name on them, and I would let the customers pinch them. People love it when they feel they are getting something for nothing. Plus, every time the guy takes a shower back home, there's your ad. I'd include the cost of the robes in the price of the room.

Next, on every floor I'd put a desk and a host or hostess by the elevator. Their function would be to greet the customers and to ensure that their every wish and whim be granted. I'd have real blankets—not those brown synthetic jobs most hotels provide. Every room would have a four-poster bed. What does it cost? It's only four poles and a bit of drape. But it *feels* regal—lovers especially like that stuff. Finally, I'd get all my staff in the parking lot at dawn, and I would have them jump up and down shouting, "The customer is always right, even when they are wrong." I'd make the staff do that until they got it, even if it took an hour every morning. Those who really couldn't get it, I'd bus to Marriott.

Life is so simple, really. Think through what people want, watch what others fail to give them, and provide it. Then bill 'em.

In the dollar-dance of life, there is one more point that I want you to focus on, for it will become vital to you as your abundance consciousness grows. The world is rich, very rich, especially the Western democracies. Now if you are reading this book, it is more than likely that you live in one of these very abundant countries. If you don't, move. To be abundant you have to hang out in dimensions that are abundant.

The point here is that people tend to focus only on what is lacking. They rarely focus on what is available or real or actually there. So, for example, in the United States at this time we have about six million people on the dole. There is a workforce of around 105 million people, which means that there are 99 million not on the dole. Those characters earn, on average, close to $20,000 per year. But many of them earn much, much more. In fact, more than a million of them are millionaires.

Let us say that we take double the national average wage as our norm, that is, $40,000, and we add up how many people in America earn that. You would be amazed to discover that there are more folk in the $40,000-plus range than there are on the dole. Meaning that for everyone who is out of work, there are many more who are experiencing abundance and actually earning double the national average.

You can apply this kind of thinking to almost any Western democracy you want to look at. Take England as another example. If you drew a line from Cambridge to Bristol, the area south of that line is just a few hundred miles square. In that hallowed spot live some of the most abundant, rich people in the world. Their wealth is vast. Collectively they own a sizable percentage of the world. Interestingly enough, they are some of the largest foreign owners of property in the United States. Now if you read the British papers, you would get the impression that everything is going down the pan and that those people are having trouble rubbing two royal pennies together. That is not the truth. "Ahh, but," would say the negative souls, "what about the north of England? It is so miserable and poor and wretched, and industry there is so depressed." And I would say to them, "True." But what is positive and lovely about the north of England is that it is not that far away. A £30 bus ride gets you over the Cambridge/Bristol line and in the thick of things. Plus, there isn't any reason why you can't make it anywhere. It's just that some spots are more conducive to abundance than others.

The ego/personality tends to want to plop on one spot and stay there, to be surrounded with what it knows, even if what it knows is not that pleasant. Yet one of the features of the wealthy is that they move around a lot. And in the same way that the abundance of nature is patchy, some places are green and plentiful, while other places are deserts. The abundance of the world tends to congregate in specific areas. Markets come and go, values rise and fall. To be a part of that nowadays you need good communications, reliable information, and a fast pair of legs.

Successful people are usually more lively than those who are unsuccessful. The quickening of the spirit they feel comes out of their creativity, and success detaches them from the more rigid outlook on life—it puts them in the flow. So the shakers and movers, by their very nature, are moving faster, taking more risks, and investing more in the world than their less active counterparts.

They have joined, so to speak. Thus, they are naturally entitled to a more fluid, more free lifestyle. Not because anyone is dishing out little merit badges of good fortune, hither and thither. But because to those who have energy, more shall be naturally added.

All you have to do is agree to join. You may have already done so. Perhaps all you need is to polish up your act and focus your intent. It is very likely that many of you are just a hairsbreadth away from the mother lode. Hang on. Don't lose heart. By being involved long enough and forcefully enough, you will discover that eventually the system delivers. Too many quit before the final payout.

In the meantime, you are going to have to work on your energy, for at this level your currency is energy, nothing more. As you raise your energy, the people show up. And by now you'll be comfortable billing 'em. It is nothing more complicated than that. As you get stronger, it gets easier and easier.

Let us press on and look at energy, and how you will raise yours.

5

Money Making Is a Piece of Cake— Chocolate Cake

What you put out is what you get back, and the reason why so many are so short of money is that they put little or nothing out. If you are truly dedicated to getting into the dollar-dance of life, you are going to have to get used to creating almost constant energy.

But before you lift a finger, let us look at the quality of energy you are putting out so that when your energy mixes with that of the marketplace of life, you will only need small amounts of what you are in order to generate large amounts in return. Otherwise, you sentence yourself to a life of grueling struggle, a life where at every turn you see evidence of how the world does not respond to, or does not accept in commercial terms, the things you have to offer.

Abundance consciousness is a piece of cake—chocolate cake. To have it is a natural part of your *modus*. We need to look at three main headings and your attitudes to those topics.

- ✦ Intellectual abundance
- ✦ Emotional/spiritual abundance
- ✦ Physical/commercial abundance

If you think of our society, you see how the older generation, coming as they do from hard times, often endorses a view that shortages are rife. All of our culture and even our sayings endorse this. A stitch in time saves nine. A penny saved is a penny earned. The meek shall inherit the earth. (I met Meek once. He's a Jewish lawyer in Philadelphia. He's richer than God.)

How many times have you heard that to make money you have to work hard? Who told you that? The people who told you were the ones who had experienced life as hard. They wanted you to experience it in the same way so that you could join them and they wouldn't get lonely. The people who try to sell you on the struggle of life are those who, by virtue of that struggle, know little about how to make it. Best not to use them as advisors.

Of course the idea that hard work and struggle are inevitable is nonsense. Inside the energy of abundance, there is no struggle, only flow. If you are struggling, there is something about your thinking or your modus that needs adjustment. Effort is a natural part of our physical state, but struggle is effort laced with emotion, and that is unnatural and unholy. You don't need it.

But it is not surprising that we do struggle, for all the institutions that control the flow of information to the people—whether it be religion, media, or bureaucracy—have to appeal to the common denominator. No politician can get up on his orange box and tell the truth like this: "This country is really abundant. Ninety-five percent are doing really well. Let's not bother too much about the deadbeats; there aren't that many of them anyway."

So a part of your abundance intellect will have to step beyond the great lies of life, the lies perpetrated by the mind-set of tick-tock. That mind-set will never agree that things are actually okay, even if they should become so. The concepts of tick-tock have to sustain a constant discomfort in order to keep everyone under control.

The institutions of the world, as well as the mind-set of the ordinary man, have a vested interest in setting their sights nice and low. That way, no one has to achieve too much in order to make it. And if they fail, they don't fail by too much either.

Imagine the leaders getting up and saying, "Hey, abundance is natural, and anyone who's not making $100,000 a year will be fined for lack of effort." That campaign slogan would go down like a brick balloon. But, in fact, metaphysically, that is actually what is happening. Those who create little or nothing are penalized by the circumstances of life, for the richness of their possibilities are taken from them. So you can create all the phony circumstances that you want, but in the end what is truth is truth. It lays there for all to see, as if someone plopped an oily Spanish omelet on your chest. It's impossible to ignore.

To become rich, you first have to accept that intellectually. You have to think rich. This is achieved in two ways. First, you never endorse a thought-form of scarcity or lack in your circumstances; and further, you never endorse the poverty of others. As a part of this change in consciousness, you begin to align and to acknowledge the richness of things. So when a fine-looking limo passes you on the freeway, rather than saying, "Capitalist lackey, must be a crook," say to yourself how nice stretch limos look and how simple they are to obtain.

In addition, it is important that you never view another person's success as an affirmation of your lack. If you hear of a friend who is doing well, it is so easy for his or her success to highlight the fact that perhaps you are doing less well. It is only a matter of intellect. If your friends are doing well, you can develop a thinking that uses their success to confirm and endorse that the world is truly a creative place to be. Their success should be encouraging, for if that "plank" can make it, so can you.

But you have to allow your thinking to expand to accept the image of absolute abundance as natural. That can be hard, as we are programmed into lack by a thousand-and-one messages that all have our lack at heart. Further, we are influenced by the constant bombardment that mediocrity offers us as truth. Not only are you the product of all the information that is going on, but you are also the product of many inputs of which you are not consciously aware.

Your mind picks up and stores all conscious events, but it is also the owner of those bits of information that it picks up subliminally. Often you are not able to consciously disagree with whatever subliminal input has entered your mind. You might be standing in the supermarket feeling abundant with a trolley full of groceries, and a person three or four aisles away picks up a can of beans, looks at it, and says, "Bloody hell! The world's falling apart. I can't afford that." Even though that comment may be up to 40 decibels below your normal earshot, it goes into your mind and can form a part of your reality.

Now it's natural for you to think that you are not influenced in your thinking by the energy of others, but the fact is, you are. Everything that you think and feel is shaped by your life's experiences, and those experiences are a reflection of whatever consciousness you held at that particular time. That consciousness was and still is the product of whatever you believe to be real. So, to say that you are not influenced by the thought of others is ludicrous, for if you were to track back and unravel each and every experience of your life, you could eventually understand what created it—and how it came from your mind. Sooner or later you would get down to how it got in there, and you would find that it came from someone else.

The average person's experience of the world is very limited. For example, only a minority of people ever travel outside of their own country, and an even smaller percentage ever visit more than, say, ten other countries. Yet everyone has an opinion about what is going on in the world even though they don't really have a clue what they are talking about. I love those surveys when they ask the man in the street what he thinks about the Persian Gulf or whatever. Sixty percent say the government is making a mess of things, 32 percent say it's doing fine, and 8 percent reply, "Don't know." I have the deepest respect for the don't knows for they are the only ones actually telling the truth. The rest are usually talking out of the back of their hat!

And so it is with abundance thinking. Everything you learned came from someone else. Most likely what you learned was extremely debilitating and tainted by the opinion of others. You took that as your reality and projected that from your consciousness. Bit by bit, the circumstances you experienced in life began to reflect whatever you believed. So you were able to underwrite those beliefs with personal experiences that confirmed to you that, say, making money is hard work.

Thus, every time you get close to making a pile of quick money, something comes along to sabotage it, and you live in a reality that falls a bit short of the final payout. Intellectually, it is often hard to understand why. Once that type of shortfall has occurred three or four times over a period of years, you are then scarred for life—unless you are very forceful in your contradiction of that energy.

💰 DOLLAR-DANCE CONCEPT 5 💰

"Because money is a major psychic symbol of security, every thought you have that endorses your insecurity affects your money-making abilities. Money flows toward stability and away from its converse."

To lay down a thinking strong enough to defend you from the bombardment of negative energy offered is not a complicated process, but it does take mental discipline. It forces you to constantly police your mind to override your own negativity and the negativity of others. If, for example, you track your thoughts for an hour each day, you will be amazed to discover that on average you will have six to ten insecurity thoughts each hour.

These thoughts can be concerns about your health or about safety or injury. They can be various worries about money. "If I leave my car here, will it get stolen?" Or they will be just various emanations of the general insecurity that the mind believes to be real. Then, while watching your thoughts carefully, notice how many of those insecurities deal with money. You will notice that the mind is constantly concerned with being ripped off or losing what it has—will there be enough? What if everything collapses, and so forth.

When you go out to make a deal and it falls apart, the mind does not understand logically why that happened. Yet, pummeled into your consciousness are hundreds or even thousands of negative inputs that fracture your confidence and ruin your psychic stability. As you bring that damaged self into the circumstances of life, it is natural that those circumstances soon reflect the same uncertainty.

It's hard for people to realize that these two aspects of their lives that seem disconnected are, in fact, interrelated. Because money is a major psychic symbol of security, every thought you have that endorses your insecurity affects your money-making abilities. Those thoughts create instability in your energy. Money flows toward stability and away from its converse.

This negative pillaging of your self-confidence gives off tell-tale signs that others pick up immediately. Those signs remind them of their own vulnerability. People won't part with their money unless they feel safe. If there is the slightest doubt, they'll head for the bushes.

To heal this aspect of your life, you have to train yourself to feel secure even if there is no evidence to suggest such to be the case. You have to settle into the uncertainty of things and be comfortable with it. Never voice negativity even if things are not going well. Your world is changing, there's always tomorrow, and all will work out fine in the end. If you have suffered a major financial setback, you can rest in the thought that you were crafty enough to make the cash in the first place. Now your energy is moving upward, and it will take you no time at all to replace that which has slipped away. Powerful consciousness about life and money is only habit. Agree to change your habits if that's what it takes. Simple, really.

To make it in life, you may have to get out there and hustle your butt, for the system is stacked against you. To become wealthy requires you to exert the force of your *will* in order to penetrate the bubble of control that surrounds us. It is a fact that the 96 percent of working Americans retire with net assets of just $400. That's mind-boggling. Of the remaining 4 percent, 2 percent retire comfortably and 2 percent have become very rich. Why is that so?

It's because at every turn, money is taken from you. You incur tax liabilities 24 hours of the day. Every move you make is taxed. The system is designed so that no one can actually find out what tax they've paid. One can't track every purchase ever made or how much tax was included in the price.

Every time a buck is taken from you, you lose the use of that dollar for life. The system sucks 40 to 50 percent of everyone's income, annually. So the government controls most of the capital. They also employ most of the people. Half the workforce is employed by the government or by companies that contract solely to the system. The government owns almost all the land—only a minute percentage is in private hands. Further, the powers that be control and regulate the market forces through which citizens have to operate. It is exactly like the Mafia. In tick-tock, people are too apathetic to push against this nonsense and become a success anyway.

The Western democracies are the freest in the world. Certainly no one would argue that the American Constitution is anything but fair, for it is the most politically sophisticated on the planet. But, although we have a good legal system and are protected by the Bill of Rights, we have little or no financial freedom.

💰 DOLLAR-DANCE CONCEPT 6 💰

"The greatest revenge is doing well."

How is the average person going to feel free and develop an abundance consciousness when the system takes half his profit and controls his every commercial move? Under these circumstances, what does democracy really do for you? You may get to vote from time to time, which is better than not having a vote, but if you can't control what the prune does when he gets to Parliament, what's the use?

What fascinates me about the American political system is that once a person takes his or her seat in Congress, he or she is rarely voted out. It's a bit like Russia. At election time many of the U.S. politicians are reelected unopposed or face no real contest. Over 90 percent are back again the following week. This is because in America there's a quaint practice whereby you can give an elected member of Congress large sums of money to win his or her affection, and that gift is not considered a bribe or illegal. Of course, it was the politicians themselves who passed this rule. Free money and, thus, power is intoxicating. No one will vote to change that. Once happily seated, the member quickly builds a vast war chest that he or she brings to bear upon opponents at election time.

The second part of this quaint practice that also boggles the mind is that when a politician retires, he or she is allowed to keep whatever sums are in that chest unspent. Many have over a million dollars tucked away for retirement day. How or why would a character thus benefited ever vote against interests that provide free money so generously? Is it the common man who provides this largess? No, it's the forces in control that need his vote and his power, not the individual.

If someone can toss a congressman a hundred grand to regulate the price of a leg of beef—so that all the common folk are paying over the top—it's natural that the forces in control would do that. What's a hundred grand, compared to an extra buck or two on every chunk of beef consumed in the country? It's not surprising that the politicians are so despised and disliked by the people. Let's face it—if your senator fell off a cliff, you might momentarily regret that it wasn't you who shoved him, but you wouldn't exactly lose a lot of sleep over his demise, would you? Of course, the politicians don't see it that way. They kid themselves that they have the people's affection—a bit as Mussolini did—and they waffle on about service and commitment, while each day they vote to bind the people further. In the end, the average guy, realizing he can't beat the system, walks away. It's not surprising that the majority of the people are politically apathetic. What other option have they got? Apathy, after all, is a quality much revered by governments, for a sleeping population doesn't read the small print. Tick-tock is then cheap to control.

Over the years, the powers that be have trussed us up by regulating and taxing our every commercial activity. No one minds contributing a bit to the pot, but over time the system has been inflated to where thousands upon thousands of regulatory agencies exist to take the fruit of our labor and ensure control over the system. You are free as a bird as long as you don't want to do anything. But if you cross the street and open a pizza parlor, 20 government officials jump into bed with you. Most independent business people in this country are basically working for the government. Half of their week is spent working for nothing to pay what is supposedly "owed" in tax, and part of the rest of the week is lost to feeding the bureaucratic behemoth its daily diet of little forms and returns.

Think of this: All the money in the world really belongs to the governments. It's theirs. They printed it, and even though they may hand out a little bit of it for us to play with, they have made damn sure they are going to get it all back eventually. What you have is only on loan from them. It can be taken from you at a moment's notice.

Most American's don't remember when Roosevelt passed laws repossessing all their gold. More recently, Mexico had a cheery little fellow called Presidente Madrid running the show. Having built himself endless palaces while his people starved, he then ran a little short. But the intrepid "Presidente" didn't let cash-flow problems spoil his fun. He nationalized all the banks and let the peso collapse, dropping from an exchange rate of 8 to the U.S. dollar to 2,400 to the dollar, where it stands today. Many hardworking Mexicans lost their life's savings overnight.

The others, having gotten wind of where Madrid was heading, began shipping their cash out of the country to the tune of billions per week. Naturally, the government newspapers called them chiselers and rats for not wanting to lose everything. Meanwhile, back in the U.S., the Congress was supporting Presidente Madrid like crazy. Our illustrious leaders had added up the difference between 8 pesos and 2,400, and suddenly they had 2,392 good excuses for shipping Madrid millions in our money to keep him on the job. The upshot for Mexico was that the capital infrastructure was destroyed as the smart money fled, and the people were impoverished even further. American businesses operating just over the border at places such as Juarez loved it. They could run an entire factory for the cost of one doughnut a week. The upshot for the American people was that illegal immigration from across the Rio Grande skyrocketed.

Social services in big cities such as L.A. came under immense pressure, denying even the taxpaying, legal citizens stuff they were entitled to. In addition, the final bill has not as yet been presented. One day the folk in Mexico are going to get sorely pissed off. When that happens, they are going to blame the U.S.—with good reason, I'd say—and they'll tear the joint apart. It's going to cost the U.S. taxpayer an arm and a leg to pop over there and fix it. You can't ignore a crazed elephant that's stomping through your garden.

It's no surprise that the average Joe doesn't really believe that the world is abundant, for he has to operate in a system that sucks the lush out of his life and leaves it a bit bare. Of course, the forces in control don't have the same problem. That is why we have a world in which many are immensely rich, while the rest are scraping by, or perhaps even doing okay, but it's hard for the average guy to wind up with any real surplus.

What to do? There is nothing you can do. The way it is, is the way it is. It's too energy-draining to get upset. You have four options. First, you could be a cog in the system and settle for that. Alternatively, you could possibly join the privileged classes and hook up to the free money, delivering coffee pots to the Pentagon at a thousand dollars a pop. Third, you could live as a "fringe dweller" and operate outside the system. Or finally, you could accept that you exist in unfavorable circumstances and make a success of it anyway. The greatest revenge is doing well.

But there is a saving grace in all this nonsense. Although the government takes half your money, it is still possible to make an untold fortune with the half they leave behind. The taxes and the regulations just delay your reaching financial freedom, but they can't stop you completely. So the name of the game is not to allow the situation to influence you too much and to head for the target no matter what. As the Romans might have said, "Non Illegitimati Carburundum" or, loosely translated, "Don't let the bastards grind you down."

In the same way that you need to feel secure even when you are not, this dimension also requires you to feel financially free in your heart when, at the beginning of your career anyway, this is not usually the case. You have to understand that there are no guarantees in life, there is no absolute security, and there is usually no simple path to financial success. It's going to take some effort. For the mind to chase after security is ludicrous: It will never get it, and the irritation of constantly seeking security destroys what stability there is.

It is simpler, therefore, to agree that one doesn't need security. One doesn't even need a system that favors one. All that is ever needed is what one already has, which is creativity and energy. You don't have to become immortal to be safe. All you have to do is to acknowledge that what you are right now is enough to keep you safe and more than enough to keep you in abundance for the rest of your days, in spite of circumstances. You just need *you*, comfortable inside yourself.

Next, move your thinking out of the mass discontent of life, and you can begin to see that the Universal Law that covers our destiny is, in fact, absolutely fair. Life is fair, even when it isn't. And although the mind of tick-tock will insist that misfortune and chance are real, that opinion, in itself, held as it is by millions, does not make it truth. It is just opinion. I appreciate that at some levels of tick-tock, people exercise almost no control over their affairs and so feel that they are abandoned to the vagaries of chance. However, there is a level of operation that lies somewhat beyond tick-tock, in which one accepts absolute responsibility for the circumstances of one's life and understands that by correctly projecting consciousness and actions onto reality, one can dominate that reality, going beyond its restrictions and moving it in any direction one wishes. The fact that a million people standing next to you don't know how to do that doesn't make you wrong and them right.

Further, projected power-of-self grants you the only security you will ever have or ever need. Then the metaphysics of the Universal Law in motion becomes fair, for you live only in a mental, emotional, and spiritual projection of who you are. So what you get is yours. Events belong to you personally, and at that level, life becomes simple, for you waste no energy or thought in wondering why this and why that. Everything is obvious. And in the natural truth of things, what to do is also obvious. Life takes on a new meaning, for you mean for it to do so.

To make a lot of money, you will have to decide to become somewhat abnormal. Normal people are rarely successful, and what success they do enjoy is often tainted by their discomfort in life. So when they make a pile of cash, it is useless to them, and in fact it often traps them deeper within the ghetto of the mind.

By abnormal, I don't mean becoming a weirdo, but merely that you take on an abundance consciousness that is different from the way most people think. What you are trying to do is to change the way you feel and operate—not only from a monetary point of view—but also in the all 'round spiritual and physical point of view from which you approach life. You are trying to become a truly independent being—abundance is one aspect of that independence. As you incorporate money making into your spiritual quest, it takes on an added impetus. Just making money for the sake of making it can become vapid and boring, but when your financial success is linked to your spiritual desire for true independence, then your money-making efforts take on a kind of holiness.

People often miss that point. It comes back to the point made earlier that people tend to think that money is not spiritual. This is because, especially in the olden days, the major religions taught that poverty was holy and that wealth was not. Years ago, when all of the major religions were getting started, society was made up of the kings, the landed gentry, and then everybody else. The religions needed members to survive, so they naturally had to appeal to the common folk, most of whom were desperately poor. In order to win the affection of the masses, poverty had to be made okay—better than okay. The poor would ask, "Hey, how come your God lets me starve?" There was no decent answer to that. So the religions promised the poor a special place in heaven, which was a bit simpler than trying to figure out how to fix everyone's desperate circumstance.

Now if you look at our planet, especially in the modern day, you can see that we live in a place that is exceptionally lush. As was said before, there is a surplus of everything. The climate is temperate; for the most part, the seas are full of richness; and there is every fuel, mineral, and chemical that we will ever need at our feet. The sun shines on our lands and grants us vast richness. There is more food than we can ever eat. There is more wealth, creativity, and resources than we can ever use up.

Now think of this: Why would God or the God-force put us in a dimension of such incredible wealth and abundance—a veritable Garden of Eden—and expect us to be poor and lacking in our needs? It makes no sense. It is natural that we would use the resources around us and gradually become abundant. God must have foreseen that as having a high probability. Given the dimension we live in, richness is natural.

To make that philosophically wrong, and to make poverty—which is so *unnatural*—right, is a conceptual flip-flop. It may serve certain vested interests, but under the Universal Law governing the naturalness of things, this cannot be truth. Imagine a God who considers the dole and food stamps holy and good, and, alternately, considers the opening of a factory that grants creativity and wealth to, say, a hundred families, wrong. You can stick that in yer ear, kid; it just ain't true!

But we bought into all this stuff, and the level to which we bought in is probably the level at which we find ourselves financially today. Understand that, for the most part, all the things you were taught as true, that you hold to so dearly in your consciousness, are probably two-thirds of four-fifths ludicrous.

However, that twaddle and weakness you took on is a gift, for it allows you to climb. It gives you a challenge to go beyond. Within the difficulty of that fractured consciousness, you can transcend and change so that your life becomes an expression of a massive energy. Your pleasure in being on a quest gives you a reason for living, which of course is a lot different from just surviving.

Thinking big and thinking rich will help you go beyond the poverty of the world, but it isn't all that you are going to need. To really develop financial power, you will probably have to exist in a reality that is separate from the status quo. The status quo is vested with keeping you and the rest of the world in line. You have to break out of that.

When you walk out into the marketplace and you look at the price of things, what you see is just a thought-form, people's opinion. It is not necessarily real. The market is established thus because in the minds of the traders taking your money it is reasonable. So, markets are always stacked slightly against the consumer. There is an unwritten agreement among the manufacturers, distributors, and retailers on how much they can charge the public and get away with it. Markets are arranged to establish and benefit the status quo.

In the town in which I live, there are about a dozen gas stations. Every station sells unleaded gasoline at exactly the same price. There's not even a tenth of a cent difference. Coincidence? Hardly. Here gas sells for approximately ten cents more per gallon than anywhere else in the state. For this arrangement to work, all the traders have to come to a special agreement, for normally it is impossible for 12 people to randomly agree on anything. So the residents who live here constantly pay over the top for their gas because the cartel sustains and defends the thought-form.

Even in free markets, prices are relatively fixed. When you go into a store and they offer you 20 percent off, it looks on the surface as if they are giving you something. But what are you getting the discount on? On the marketplace thought-form. Price is a product of emotion. There is no real worth to anything. But the

markets are maneuvered in such a way that once a price is established over time, that opinion or thought-form becomes rigid. To
challenge the established "opinion" is considered a heresy and a
threat to survival. There is usually an adverse reaction if you dare
to combat what is often an emotional manipulation of the paying
public. This is because once a price or a market practice has been
established by repetition, that price enters the minds of those
engaged in the market almost as a God-given right. It becomes
part of the overall pattern that guarantees survival. They consider it reasonable, so contradicting the status quo is taboo.

If, for example, you went over to your neighbor's house on
Friday at noon and gave him $1,000, he would be delighted. Let
us say you repeated this gift every Friday for nine weeks. In
doing so, you establish a status quo in his emotions. By now your
neighbor has budgeted the free money into his overall plan. On
the tenth Friday, without saying a word, you decide not to make
the gift, so you don't show up. Your decision would cause a negative reaction. More than likely he would call you a communist
and a rat, for you have tampered with his survival mechanism.

You can't go out and bitch at the price of a candy bar. In
doing so you would destroy your equilibrium. But you can, from
time to time, challenge the norm as a way of affirming that your
reality is just as valid as anyone else's. In my seminars, I ask the
participants to go into a store, pick a fairly high-priced item, a TV
set perhaps, and then bid the storekeeper about 20 percent of the
sticker price.

Try it. Do it every day for a week or two until you feel comfortable pressing against the bubble. The exercise teaches you
two things: It affirms your self-image, and it allows you to practice emotional detachment as the storekeeper jumps up and down.
There's his TV, all gleaming and shiny with an $800 thought-
form printed on a little card. And you turn, look him straight in
the eye, and say, "Thank you, I'll take it. Here's $160, all cash!"

The next two minutes are a metaphysical pantomime, second

to none. As soon as you make the offer, start counting out the money. The storekeeper's first thought will be that you must be joking. While counting out the cash, look down. That defends you from the psychic power of his reaction. Regardless of what he says, continue to act as if it is a done deal, and toss in a question about whether he offers free delivery or not. By pushing through with these follow-up actions, you confirm your thought-form, which is, *Give me this TV for 160 bucks.* His reaction will be fairly predictable. Take no notice. Walk over to the TV, and smiling, lift it off the counter. By following up your low offer with action, you are metaphysically trying to penetrate a thought-form, rather than just challenging it. If the shopkeeper reacts negatively, watch and see how *you* react. We are trained to follow along like sheep. When you don't, your childhood memories flood back from the subconscious, and you feel that you are naughty and a lousy person for even daring to suggest a discount of 80 percent. Retain your poise.

When you get really sophisticated at this game, try this: Go to a restaurant with a few friends, have a lovely meal, and order everything. When the waiter brings over the check, refuse to pay. Say in a loud voice so that everyone can hear, something such as, "I didn't think the meal was that good. The potatoes were a bit cold." Get your friends to back you up. It takes a certain force of *will* to pull this off because legally you are dead wrong. But strategically you have the high ground, because the restaurant can't repossess the product.

The exercise here is to sustain an opinion that contradicts the norm and to defend that opinion, without emotion. You are not trying to be combative. You are just practicing holding a view that is diametrically opposed to the status quo.

Niggling the status quo is a lot of fun. Even though you may not get the meal for free, you will usually come away with a hefty discount. By pressing the bubble, you affirm your self-image, which is a vital key to money making. But also, it allows you to remember that your reality is as valid as, if not more so than, everyone else's. It trains you to stand your ground.

Bit by bit, your thinking moves from tick-tock into an unusual originality. Critical thinking, it's called. When you find yourself in a business situation, you will have trained your mind to see a dozen possibilities that no one else notices. Standing outside the norm allows you creative freedom that you can turn into cash.

But as abundance thinking starts to become natural, there are several points you may need to watch. Thinking big is fine, and it often brings you big results. But in its bigness there is also the propensity to collapse. Allow me to explain.

Let us say that the level at which you operate at this time is a hundred thousand a year. So now you are beginning to think in terms of a million. In the journey from a hundred thousand to a million, you will have to stay balanced and patient and concentrate on day-to-day things so that eventually you look up from your work and there is a million.

However, often people who endorse thinking big have a tendency, first, to get out ahead of themselves, and, second, to drift into fantasy. When their imagination takes them out beyond what is controllable, things tend to fall apart. As you climb, you have to concentrate, for in climbing, your propensity for imbalance is greater. If your mind is way out ahead of you, current events and responsibilities tend to be ignored and—lacking the empowerment of your concentration—often unravel.

Anytime you find yourself in transition, you should be aware that in moving from A to B, you need additional balance and an even more centered concentration. The circumstances that you are familiar with—let us say, the $100,000 level—you can control and dominate because you are used to them. But as you move toward the million-dollar level, circumstances change, and you will have to adapt to them gradually, developing an energy within you that can control circumstances that are ten times bigger.

💰 DOLLAR-DANCE CONCEPT 7 💰

"Concentrate on what you know or on what works. Don't allow the lure of activity to take you beyond what is comfortable and controllable."

Often you will see a person develop a good idea. He opens a pizza shop and makes a success of that. Then the fellow tries to expand, so he then opens three more shops, usually on borrowed money. The new units take all of his energy, and the original shop starts to falter. He is now working 16 hours a day, and in the massive effort that that takes, he is thrown even farther off balance.

At this point, our man becomes mesmerized by his own activity. He decides that ten million is where he ought to be, so he opens a wholesale food trucking company, even though he knows little or nothing about that type of business. Suddenly, four trucks are hauling tomatoes through the night, and the fellow is pleased with himself. Now he can work 24 hours a day and really feel that his contribution is worthwhile. Meanwhile, pizza shop number one disintegrates, while in shop two the manager is weeding the takings. Then the tomato business takes a nosedive, and one day our man looks up to view two tons of salami about to land on his head. It's over.

The trick to thinking big is to allow your mind to carry you up, up, and away, while your eyes are firmly focused down at your feet. Concentrate on what you know, or on what works. Don't allow the lure of activity to take you beyond where you feel comfortable and in control. Remember, there is no rush. You can get to a million in six months, or you can get there in six years. It won't make that much difference to you as long as you are balanced and enjoying life on the way.

In fact, going slowly and savoring life as you go allows you to grant the journey more meaning. To hurtle along at breakneck speed is at times fun. But it ought to be tempered with times of standing still, of evaluating what has been created, and of taking time to develop controls so that future efforts are not plunked on a rickety foundation.

The final point about abundance consciousness and thinking big is to remember that the mind does not believe in its own fantasy. It is used to wandering around, imagining all sorts of things that it knows are not real. This is one of its entertainments. So if your fantasies overrun you, your mind indulges itself in that and fails to empower or concentrate on what is mundane but real. Gradually, the ego/personality devalues what you are involved in right now and carries you out into a fantasy projection of the intellect. The result is that you become dissatisfied with what you are and what you have and start to concentrate almost exclusively on what you don't have.

As you concentrate only on the unreal, it becomes more and more unobtainable, for the mind knows that you are not serious in your quest. Your thoughts are just daydreams, and each and every one of them serves as an affirmation that you consider your projections and goals to be unattainable. This gradually disengages you from those goals, and you spiral downwards into stagnation. The energy of what you do have is neither empowered nor acknowledged by your mind, so bit by bit its liveliness is used up. What you see around you becomes empty and lifeless. Then, trying to move from the self-created dead zone into your fantasies becomes almost impossible. Unless, of course, your consciousness is prepared to do a 180-degree turn, which often it won't.

As things become dead, apathy and negativity set in. Then enthusiasm for your quest dribbles away and is lost, partly to failure and often to confusion. Past successes are forgotten, current setbacks are made to seem ever more real, and eventually what you believe to be true about your life becomes set. As your energy gradually drops, you find yourself back in tick-tock and look down to find that it has you by the short and curlies.

Be warned. Expansion is desirable, but it is also destructive. When taken gradually, in comfort, it's a joy and delight to behold. If taken too fast, the spirit becomes overwhelmed and eventually discovers a way to disencumber itself. So you go bankrupt or die, or your quest self-destructs. You don't need that.

Look at the economic history of the world since the Second World War. Things have expanded like crazy. It didn't matter if we had the money to pay for that expansion or not. We have bred a society that is restless, that constantly wants more. So our governments churn out paper money to keep everyone happy. No one cares that a post-war dollar is now worth only four cents. All that imbalance will have to be dealt with someday. Expansion without control is a sure way of inviting collapse.

If you have a good idea, perfect it even further. Then from that microcosm, carry it forward into the macro-sphere. Repeat the format over and over again. Then bam! Suddenly you have 800 hamburger joints. Pure tick-tock, really, but you have to join in order to get out: The only way beyond tick-tock is through it. While traveling through, you can disengage your thinking from the common consciousness and operate in a way that tick-tock will appreciate. But you will think in a way that is free and personal to you.

As you tromp through, heading toward your final liberation, you will have to agree to take responsibility for things, including, of course, yourself. There are few wealthy people who do not accept responsibility naturally. If you have avoided it in your life, you may want to focus on how much responsibility you are prepared to take. For although on the surface responsibility seems an encumbrance to be avoided, poverty is an even greater drag.

Taking responsibility is only a trap if your emotions are wrapped up in that responsibility. There is a way of being responsible for vast amounts of things and not to be particularly emotionally involved. That, of course, takes self-confidence. It seems to me that the main reason why people won't take responsibility is that they lack confidence or are scared or feel that if they commit to something, they will be trapped in it for life. None of this is necessarily true. It will always depend on how you look at things.

If you are not comfortable taking responsibility, then just put this book down for a moment and agree with yourself that you will take responsibility, whether you are comfortable with it or not. Otherwise, you sentence yourself to perpetual struggle. Further, you don't have to take on vast chunks at one time. Accept responsibility for, say, one or two new things. Complete those satisfactorily, acknowledge that you did so and that it was a breeze, really, and then open yourself up for a bit more.

To be responsible for a small amount and to be responsible for a large amount is no different, really. Both take your concentration and dedication—the difference being that when you agree to be responsible for many things, you earn more. So if you are prepared to be responsible for anything at all, you might as well elect for something huge, for in the end it will serve you better.

If you agree to manage one hamburger joint, you might as well agree to look after 800. For while managing one will never set you free, accepting responsibility for all 800 will. And to get into that position of responsibility, you have only to agree with your mind that you will accept that. Just put it into your consciousness that you are prepared to accept more and more responsibility, and sooner or later it shows up. Taking responsibility is not a position many enjoy. So if one in a crowd calls out for it, everyone else is happy to dump as quickly as they can. When they load the responsibilities on you, smile, and then bill 'em.

💰 **DOLLAR-DANCE CONCEPT 8** 💰

"As you tromp through, heading toward your final liberation, you will have to agree to take

responsibility for things, including—of course—
yourself. There are few wealthy people who do not
accept responsibility naturally."

The next key to abundance thinking that we ought to consider is commitment. This quality goes hand in hand with responsibility. Often you will find that creative people have a reluctance to commit or to join. They feel that if they do so, their creativity will be hamstrung, so they never get into the marketplace of life properly. Later in this book, we will discuss the number-one key to success, which I call "concerted action in the marketplace." Suffice it to say that if you want to get ahead in life or just make a little bit more, you will have to first commit to that in your thinking. In other words, it has to become important to you.

It is pointless to say that you want a little more and to not feel too sure about whether you want it or not. If you want more, you will have to commit energy to that idea, energy you will swap for cash. That often means that the hustle and bustle of the marketplace will call on you to get in a little deeper than you currently are. It may mean more work or more responsibility, as discussed, or just more concentration on what it is that you are doing. But all of that begins with the mental idea that you will commit to the goal.

Often you will hear people bemoan their financial state, and in the very same breath they will tell you that they are not interested in money. It is true that many people are genuinely not interested in becoming wealthy, and I don't have a problem with that. Many are happy to muddle along, provided they have plenty of time off for fishing or whatever. But if you have decided you want more, then you will have to energize that idea. To just say, "I would like to win the lottery" doesn't usually work, for the level of energy and enthusiasm at which that thought is conceived says by its very nature that you are prepared to do little or nothing to advance your financial status. Now if you were to say, "I want more. I am committed and dedicated to having more. I will increase my energy and my output by 50 percent, and I will also buy some lottery tickets," then suddenly you have a plan that will work.

By now, you may have developed a higher consciousness and gone beyond the mindless rhythm of tick-tock, but it is important to remember that in order for you to translate that higher consciousness into cash, you will most likely have to return to the land of tick-tock in order to sell what you have. As you reenter, you will have to respect the normal workings of things. You will have to play the game and follow the rules. If you don't, then you will alienate the very people who are just on the verge of transferring their cash to you. And whereas you may in your mind be coming from a totally different perspective, you will have to play along in order not to sabotage your plans. So as a part of your commitment you will have to agree to join the system, if only for a limited period. It is hard to get into the big money without joining. Not impossible, but hard.

Let us say you are a good rock 'n' roll singer, and you are doing little gigs for a few hundred a night. To get into the real money, you will need a recording contract. That means that someone somewhere will have to lay out a bunch of cash in order to back you to make records. Your best move is a large record company rather than a little one. As you walk in the door, you will be faced with the corporation: accountants, lawyers, sales managers, PR people, and so on. You will have to play along. Even though your creativity may cause you to feel that you don't belong, at that point you'd better commit to joining. If your energy is too abrasive or too deprecating of the system, the record company backs off. They don't want to lay out several hundred thousand to get into an emotional/financial zoo.

Often creative people, because of their talent, tend to feel that they don't belong. So they become terrorists. They criticize and destroy at every turn. Then as they try to market their creativity, they are faced with people's negative reactions. They find that that every time they are on the verge of the big money, something happens to spin them out.

The point to remember is that to get beyond life, you have to join, and as you join, you have to be careful to respect the thought-forms or dimensions of those who will assist you in your final liberation. That means disciplining yourself so that you can be in the system long enough to collect.

Of course, there are all sorts of places of mega-abundance that are totally outside the system. But much of the fringe is illegal. Of those activities that are honest, you'll find that, because they are fringe areas, the amount of money there is sometimes limited.

One thing you will find as you approach the big money is that sitting there on the pot are a lot of characters who have been there a long time. They are usually older in years, conservative, and set in their ways. To get them on your side, you have to be committed to yourself and your ideas. Otherwise they get jumpy, and you have to be committed to *them*. Making them wrong to their face just because they hold the reins is a fatal mistake. As you climb from, say, $100,000 to $300,000, you can more or less do as you like, but in the ascent from there to $1,000,000 and beyond, you will have to play the game.

If you go out and borrow, say $5,000, no one really cares if you are loony or not, provided they are fairly sure of getting their $5,000 back. But as you approach the million-dollar league, the potential loss in backing you is enormous. Plus, the kind of people you will be dealing with will, by the very nature of their position on the pot, be very, very rich.

Now, most people think that the rich live a relaxed, indolent life with few cares or concerns. This is far from the case. The more money you have, the more the rest of the world will be sniping at you, trying to get it from you. One of the complaints you hear from the wealthy is that they feel oppressed by the fact that everybody wants something from them. So as you approach, you had better give the impression of being committed and stable, otherwise you'll be faced with a lot of rejection.

In passing—and nothing to do with commitment—let me offer you a couple of good tips on how to deal with people who are very wealthy. Given that the wealthy are constantly under some kind of pressure in that everyone wants something from them, the way to approach them is to genuinely not want anything at all other than their company. As they get to know you, they will trust you, and the fact that you don't want anything will make you refreshingly different. It is possible that they may offer you their advice or their support, but when they do, it will be their idea, not yours. That allows you to come from strength, and it allows them to feel more relaxed about your presence.

The other thing you'll find helpful is that many wealthy people became so because they felt a need to have an impact on the world. They sought acceptance and a greater meaning to life, so they embarked on a course of action that made them rich. What they discovered, often to their chagrin, is that all the money in the world will not win them one iota of acceptance if they don't accept themselves. What they want is for you to relate to them as real people, not as a $50 million bank balance.

Further, they don't need fawning followers who are an energy drain. They need genuine friends who give them energy, acknowledgment, encouragement, and who are fun to be with. No matter how little money you have, when in the company of the very wealthy, come off as being equal to them. Treat them as equals, with respect, and they will ignore what you have and what you don't have—they will treat you as an equal, also. At that point, you will have declared yourself in, and they will have won a genuine friend.

Personally, I find the company of those of my mates who are very rich a lot of fun. For all of them are real characters who have done things in life. They are interesting, and I enjoy learning from them. When you are genuinely not focused on their money, they relax and let you into their scene. The main benefit of being in their company is that it allows you to create a feeling, an understanding, that what they are is not at all different from what you are. And if they went out and made $50 million in two years, so can you. Further, these characters are usually in the thick of things, and by just being there with them, a certain energy rubs off. So, whereas they may not be prepared to write you a check over dinner, if you stay awake, you won't need it anyway. For during the coffee and the port, the conversation drifts to the performance of ABC Finance, Inc. And the major shareholder, who is sitting across from you, twiddling his coffee spoon, happens to mention that ABC is about to quadruple its profits, double its dividend, and announce a two-for-one stock split. Bingo!

So much of abundance thinking is setting yourself up in your mind to be in the right place at the right time with the right information. Nothing more—for making money has very little to do with hard work. Well, hard work is one way, but there are lots of simpler ways. As you crank up how you think of yourself in relation to money, you will begin to watch those areas where the abundance lies, and you will get used to reading the energy of situations and placing yourself there slightly ahead of the pack. That allows you instant reward.

In conclusion, thinking abundantly is just a habit. And as you expand the circle of possibilities that you allow yourself, bit by bit the Universe responds. The reason why abundance thinking is the vital first step is that it is from the collective energy of those thought-forms that you create an overall *feeling* within you. And it is that feeling—namely, that abundance is natural to you—which pulls to you the opportunities you need in life.

"Where the moola is, someone waits for me."

✦ ✦ ✦

Feeling Rich and Lovin' It

I have always found that the metaphysical approach to life and to making money is the most empowering way to go. Perhaps you agree with me or perhaps you have another system that works just as well if not better. My point is not to try to convince you that my approach is right, but merely to have you look to see if the metaphysical approach offers you some additional benefit or insight into life.

But whatever your opinion, one thing is fact: The events of your life are created by you, and those events come to you through your feelings. Meaning that the events you experience will be exactly congruent with the sum total of whatever feelings you sustain and put out.

People who have worked upon themselves, who have truly looked within their hearts, are aware, in intimate detail, of every aspect of their feelings. They know who they are, and they constantly review how they feel about things so that they might learn more about the nature of reality and the way to control it. Unconscious people tend to negate their feelings and look instead outwards, into reality, for a meaning to life. They will hold, say, negative feelings about black people, and those feelings will be with them for years.

Because that opinion becomes a permanent part of their feelings, all positive experiences with black people will be ignored, and all negative ones will be heightened and remembered. Then one day they are stopped at the traffic light in their brand-new Mercedes when a black lady in a pickup truck rams them in the back-end and fires their Merc into the side of the Laundromat. Logically, they can't understand why it happened, and they will say, "I had a very unlucky day today. I was innocently stopped at the light when this totally out-of-control, irresponsible black lady rammed me into the Laundromat. It took 12 firemen three hours to cut me out of the spin dryer."

Of course the pickup driver has a completely different view of events. She says, "I woke up this morning with a feeling that I ought to do more to serve the local community. So I decided to take a day off from running my international cosmetics empire and drive downtown to see what's happening in town. As I walked into my six-car garage, I had this intuitive feeling not to take my Cadillac convertible. Instead, I chose the old pickup, the one with the cast-iron front fender. I don't know why I chose that; it just seemed the right decision at the time.

"As I was cruising down Main Street, I came upon a fellow in a Mercedes whose feelings needed concrete proof that black people are weirdos, so I rammed him into the Laundromat as part of my affirmation of wanting to serve humanity. I could have shoved him into the bus stop, but I thought that the Laundromat would be more symbolic of his need to clean up his act. My desire to help having been satisfied, I went home and sat in the garden, thinking how wonderful life is."

As we engage our intellect in trying to understand life, we are confronted with all sorts of events that defy logical explanations. Yet isn't it strange that in spite of these constant reminders that life is not always logical, we still have millions of people who insist that it ought to be. You would think that once they had been faced with, say, a dozen illogical situations, they'd finally give up and accept that there are patterns to life that defy logic. But no, they hold to their rigid intellectual approach, hoping that perhaps the problem of "not understanding" will be solved at a later date.

In finances, especially, you can see all sorts of patterns that intellectually make no sense. Yet everything happens for a reason. So whereas the explanation of things may not seem obvious to the intellect, it may lay there as clear as day to the *feelings* or the intuition. If you look at the successful people whom you know, often you can't put your finger on why they are doing so well. It will seem to you that they are not that clever or even that talented. Somehow, whatever they turn their hand to becomes gold. Everywhere they go, people respond to them like magic.

Of course the answer lies not so much in what those people do as in the way they feel. By being sure of themselves, being powerful and positive and allowing little to distract them, they dedicate themselves to what is, to that which is real, to that which grants them pleasure and benefits their quest. Their life is empowered through their concentrating on it, and that concentration comes out as enthusiasm, charisma, a genuine *joi-de-doin'it*. Bit by bit, their feelings begin to correspond to all those positive traits. Eventually their quest naturally exudes success, so much so that they are not consciously aware that they are doing it. They just get up each day and feel alive, well, a part of all things. Then the telephone rings and another win is tossed in the bag. It is no surprise to them, for they expect it. They understand their world and live in it as the dominant force. As such, they naturally expect things to flow their way. They use their intuition to avoid situations and people who would adversely affect that flow.

💰 DOLLAR-DANCE CONCEPT 9 💰

"You have a divine right to choose whom you will play with and under what circumstances. By eliminating any energy drag, the positive things in your life will resonate faster and faster."

The reason why money is so spiritually important to those of you on a quest is that it gives you instantly quantifiable feedback as to where your energy actually is, at this moment. That is why so many of the so-called *spiritual* folk are so phony. In pretending to hate the idea of money, living as they do away from it and negating it whenever possible, they can more easily kid themselves about achieving living sainthood.

You can see the dichotomy between that which the mind believes and that which is real very clearly in relation to money trips. It is easy for one's intellect to be diametrically opposed to one's *inner feeling*. That is why people think in terms of becoming abundant and years later are still potless. To achieve maturity as a person and make your money harvesting fruitful activities, you have to be aware of your feelings, and those feelings have to have *wealth* firmly embossed on them.

Otherwise, your money-making efforts are constantly hampered by what you actually believe in the *inner* you. That is why I say that the trick to money is having some. For once you have a little wealth, that of itself becomes an affirmation of your success, and, further, having a few bob allows you to pull out of any negative emotion around finances.

If you don't have any money, it is still a simple process to create in your feelings an acknowledgment that what you do have is abundance and that the world is, in fact, an abundant place to be. As you begin to affirm *having* rather than *not having*, bit by bit your feelings pull you into places where having is natural and suddenly you get it. Not just in your consciousness, but also literally.

Returning for a moment to the ESP of money, you can see how, as you change your feelings, free money or easy money becomes a natural part of your expectancy. In reading the energy of people and circumstances, it is simple for you to shun the hard stuff and accentuate the simple deals. To get used to using your feelings, try this exercise. Write down the names of all the major players in your life. Then, in a meditative state, imagine yourself touching them with your hand in the area of their heart. That connects you. Then feel within your own heart what energy they give off. Your first impression is usually correct, the *inner you* knows. It cannot lie. Keep it simple. Decide solely whether their energy brings you "up" or brings you "down." Write your conclusion by their name. Next, write down as titles all the major moves you are currently making in the area of finances. Visualize them in your mind's eye, and extend your hand into the middle of the events. If there are people involved, touch them. Again, write down, "up" or "down." Then look at your list, and give yourself 60 days to get rid of all the "downs." Invite all the "ups" to lunch within the next month.

You have a divine right to choose whom you will play with and under what circumstances. By eliminating any energy drag, the positive things in your life resonate faster and faster. It is easier to destroy than to create, so one "down" is not equal to one "up." It tends to cancel the up and leave you with nothing. By discarding the downs, the ups are left free-standing, solid as rocks all around you.

Of course, developing that solid, resonating feeling of *wealth* means that you will have to go beyond fear around money. For any sustained fear that is held in your feelings for any length of time will quickly unravel any positive benefits you may have created through your affirmations of wealth. It's a catch-22, really, for somehow you have to go beyond the uncertainties while you are still uncertain.

Again, whatever lack or uncertainty has been there will only be a matter of your opinion. How much effort it takes for you to change that opinion is up to you and will depend on circumstances, your upbringing, and a hundred and one other things. But once you see that wealth is only an *opinion*, an opinion that all wealthy people hold, then it is simple for you to incorporate the same, first in your thinking and then in your feelings. Once you have *joined* in your feeling, it is easy to see what separates the winners from the others.

Now, as you begin to change how you feel, you will have to watch your each and every move carefully. At the beginning, you may tend to overanalyze your life, but that is not a mistake. For in looking at every minute detail, you compensate for the fact that perhaps in the past you looked at little or none of it. Once you have a good, solid grip on who you are and what you believe, then change becomes a gradual, pleasing process where each advance generates momentum for the next.

The symbology of how you *feel* about abundance lies all around. If you look at the quality of your lifestyle, you can soon see whether or not you believe in abundance. I don't mean, how rich are you? What I mean is, do the things around you have quality and creativity; or are they drab, ugly, and dead? You can live in one room in the back end of town and still be surrounded by abundance.

Looking for the way things *feel* shows who you are. Also, it shows you quite dramatically whether or not you invest in yourself. This is vital, for it says, I believe in myself, I will spend to better myself. If you don't, others pick up on that, and that, in itself, devalues what you are in their minds. Further, it is hard to ask others for their backing and support if you won't back yourself.

The point about *feeling* is that every part of your life has to be congruent with whatever it is you wish to become. You can't expect abundance to find you if you are surrounded by the symbols of lack, for every rusty bathtub in the yard says, "No abundance here, please."

It is better, therefore, that you surround yourself with a few good-quality things than pile your life up with junk. I don't mean that you can't take advantage of a bargain if offered, but centering only on the cheap and shoddy allows you to rest *only* in that. One good pair of expensive shoes is better than a dozen pairs made underwater by Brazilian convicts at two bucks each.

If you don't have wealth at present, then you will have to adopt an air that says you are in the state of becoming more wealthy—moving up. I don't mean for you to spend a whole lot of money you don't have, lining your toaster with mink or whatever. But rather, that you should begin to seek and enjoy the quality things of life, many of which cost little or nothing. You can go to the most expensive hotel in town and just sit there and watch the hotshots trot back and forth. It won't cost you a penny. If the waiter bugs you, order a coffee and drink it slowly. When after three hours he asks if you'll have another, you reply, "No, thanks. I like to drink slowly. Anyway, I'm trying to give up caffeine."

It is interesting to me that quality items often don't cost very much more than the tacky stuff. Especially when you factor in that they last longer and give off a good feeling that enhances who you are. Yet, so often, the up-market commodities tend to put us off, for we don't immediately see what it is that we get for our money. This is because we are not taught to acknowledge a thing's intrinsic *energy* as a part of its value. Or sometimes we fear that we'll be lumbered with a bill we can't afford.

Let me give you an example. At most airports in the U.S. there are ranks of Yellow Cabs that will take you downtown for $30 to $40, depending on the distance. The drivers are usually dead sleazy, extremely negative, and the cabs feel, on an energy level, like a mortuary on a hot day with the refrigeration turned off.

Also, at most airports there is a stretch limo service. Now, most would never think of calling for a chauffeured limousine because they presume that it costs a fortune. The fact is that often it doesn't cost much more than a regular cab.

For example, at the Dallas-Fort Worth airport, a cab down-town these days will cost you around $30, while a limo costs $35. You might as well lay out the extra five dollars, ride in style, and arrive feeling good, in the care of a driver who respects and looks after you, than commit your life to some sleazebag who will hur-tle you across town in a tin can and insult you free of charge. Funny thing about the Yellow Cab system—for years I was con-vinced that it was a halfway house used to rehabilitate mutants! Of course not all urban cabbies are revolting, but many are, so why enter the crapshoot?

As you seek out excellence and quality, you naturally change the feelings around you. It is as if by acknowledging beauty, your life becomes more beautiful. To achieve this, you might have to move up-market a bit, for it is too much a stretch of the imagina-tion to see constant beauty in a dump. But as you raise your ener-gy and polish up your act, every aspect of what you are gives off a telltale sign, and people notice that, either consciously or sub-consciously.

As you move up in your feelings, you will feel better about yourself, and you'll be able to charge more. That of itself is an affirmation of how you feel, and sooner or later you'll be deal-ing only with a better class of customer. You'll do less work for more money.

Now, put this book down for a moment and agree with your-self to double your prices. Once you are happy with that, take a moment to acknowledge that abundance is just a thought-form, and that you have just incorporated a really nice money-making idea into your consciousness. Things are on the up and up....tee hee!

If you are not happy with doubling your prices, then tack 20 or 30 percent on and see how that feels. The first reaction for some will be fear, for they feel that if they put their prices up, they'll be out of a job or their product or service will be rejected. That is a natural reaction, and if you are coming from the same energy as before, it's a possibility. The way to make the price-doubling affirmation work is to begin to put more and more energy or value into whatever it is that you are doing. Then double your prices.

Whatever you are selling, whether it be your labor, expertise, product, or service, you can make it better. I am sure that if we looked carefully at what you do, we could probably see aspects that are negative or lifeless and other parts that are less than excellent. There are bound to be things that can be improved. Further, almost everything one sees in the marketplace of life is dull and boring. You can use your inventive mind to imbue your efforts with creativity and life. When you invest enthusiasm in your creativity and make things stimulating and unusual, people respond, for the public knows that 99 percent of things out there are dull and no real fun. When they discover a singing plumber, it's a joy and delight to them.

Imagine that you have a plumbing service, your van is immaculate, all of your tools are polished, and your uniform is starched and spotless. Imagine that you always arrive on time or even ten minutes early. Imagine that you actually know what you are doing, that you work at a fast and steady pace, and that you complete jobs on time. Let us say that you are available to fix leaks at any hour of the day or night, and that as you work you sing arias from *La Traviata*. Imagine that the singing is beautiful and inspires people. Imagine that you really consider the client's needs and are positive, helpful, informative, and polite. What if your service had a portable phone so that whenever a customer calls, you could answer their inquiry immediately?

Now if the other plumbers charge $30 per hour, wouldn't people pay more for your service? You can be damned sure they would. Your service is unusual and cheap—a ticket to the opera is $45. It's worth it to the customers to pay a little extra not to have to go through the hassle and emotion of hiring the regular service and having them not show up. Plus, if they don't like

La Traviata, you have a hundred tunes from the greatest musicals of all time up your sleeve. "What would you like, madam? *Oklahoma, The Sound of Music, Cats, Evita?* You name it, I'll sing it. On top of that, the water level in the front room will be down two feet in three minutes. Leave it to me. You go to the hairdressers. I'll call you when I've finished.

It is all so simple. It is only *feeling*. That feeling is empowered by your concentrating on your work. If you have the talent, use it. Make it special, and your plumbing service will be inundated with customers. You see, you can do what you want in life as long as you are different. Once you come from an energy that is unusual, people don't quantify your efforts so much in terms of money. This is because they have nothing with which to compare you. Also, they can't quantify or price what you are worth to them because most of your worth is a *feeling*, and that feeling generates in people a positive emotional response that lies outside the marketplace, and its value is whatever anyone thinks it's worth.

Let me give you one more example. There is a dry cleaning store in London whose motto is, "We clean to a standard, not to a price." When you go into their shop, it's like no other dry cleaning shop you've ever seen. There is no counter, no rows of smelly chemical clothes on wire hangers, no cash register, no tacky ads on the wall offering invisible mending. In fact, it looks like a very elegant front room. There are fine chairs and polished tables, with the latest fashion magazines, flowers, paintings, and quality carpets.

You sit down with a smelly ol' shirt in your hand, and a fellow comes out all dressed up in a formal suit and asks you if your shirt has any special requirements. Then he hauls your laundry out to the back and gives you a receipt. You can imagine their prices! But what you get is immaculate service, and everything in the store resonates and affirms quality and care. You know that your shirt is special to them and that you are special. They make you feel like it's an honor for them to become custodians of your grubby gear for a day or two. Is the store successful? Of course. It's packed.

I am sure that by now you are picking up on the excitement of feeling good about yourself and translating that into abundance feelings that will resonate from deep within you to create a more lush and harmonious lifestyle. As you begin to see the abundance of the world inside your heart, that recognition and alignment allows for an expansion of what you are—not only in cash flow terms, but also in spiritual terms. For as you accept that the supply of goodness is limitless, you begin to see yourself in limitless terms. Your overview moves gradually from little and finite, to massive and infinite.

It is as if when you let go of the emotion that surrounds your life, then life itself moves inside your heart, rather than events seeming to exist *outside* of you. It is as if you become bigger than life, rather than living in the feeling that life is outside of you and that you are at the mercy of circumstances. The first step to internalizing reality is, of course, to take absolute responsibility for yourself and for the events of your life. Doing so, you enter into an intimate relationship with the symbology of your life, and you are able to identify how that symbology relates to some *inner* feeling you hold. For example, if you feel infinite and a part of all living things and you watch a bird fly, that bird flies in your heart. You can feel it. Every subtle shift of its wings has an impact on you. You become the bird, and it is you.

Once that feeling of being larger than life has settled into your heart, your insecurities melt. Both of those aspects move hand-in-hand, being interrelated. At first, it's hard for you to see yourself larger than life, for we were brought up to allow the world to tow us by the nose. Our children are taught that they are victims of fate. However, the more you expand that feeling of infinity within, the more you go beyond fate. Then feeling yourself to be infinite, the world shrinks and you can dominate your life.

Twenty years ago, a friend gave me a gift of a small model of the world set inside an onyx cube. For a while I carried it with me everywhere I went. I will never forget it. It helped me remember that the world is really very small and that life is on that little world. To be larger than that image was not hard. When next you meditate, see the planet Earth in the palm of your hand. Imagine all the people on that little earth. Then take that image and place it in your heart. Enliven it by seeing it orbit 'round the sun. Before long, the world and its events shrink to their real size, and you expand to fill out the infinity that you really are.

Eventually you reach the point where you *know* that everything is in flow and that what you are is perfect, even though you may have imperfections. And you understand that by being in tune with the *flow* of life, you will always be in the right place at the right time. Your quality of life is guaranteed by the very fact that you can accept things as they come and that you feel in control. So your life manifests that control effortlessly and naturally.

As a final point to abundance in *feelings*, let us look for a moment to the feelings of holding on and of letting go. This may enter into the realm of pure metaphysics, but it is a vital understanding, especially as you become more and more sophisticated in the way you wield your consciousness in order to materialize the things you want.

In *The Force*, I wrote that if someone asks you for something you should give it to them. Perhaps I should have qualified that, for it caused a certain amount of confusion. The concept runs like this: If you truly feel that you are a part of all things and that life is inside of you, rather than outside of you, then all of the abundance of the world becomes yours *in feeling*, although it may not all be available to you right now as fact. Thus, being able to feel that you are everything and that everything is you allows you an attitude of infinite possibility so that you can receive limitless quantities from anywhere at any time. To enter into that kind of receiving, you have to adopt an attitude that is flowing, not bind-ing, in relation to the things that you *do* own. Meaning that, whereas you may have certain possessions that are useful and pleasing to you, if you surround those possessions with an emotion of holding on, it cuts you off from the flow and the unrestrained feeling that says abundance is everywhere and things come to me naturally and effortlessly.

The idea of releasing and not holding on does not mean that in that releasing you have to become imbalanced. For example, if you have two thousand in the bank and you have commitments for that same amount in the next week, and someone asks you for the money, you don't have to give it to them. There is no need for you to become imbalanced to be in the flow, for that very imbalance would throw you out of the flow.

All the possessions you have are basically on rental from the God-force. They will all be released eventually, either because you die and have no further need for them or because you use them up or dispose of them to another. Many of those items form a part of your needs, and to give them away could cause a problem. For example, if someone admires your trousers, does that mean you have to release them on the spot and go home on the bus in your undies? No, that may cause you a certain imbalance. But if you have 60 pairs of trousers in your closet and someone asks you for a pair, give them one. For at that moment in time, that pair of trousers does not fall into the category of an immediate need. And coming as you do from not holding on, you can release that item of clothing as a part of an affirmation that says that the abundance of the God-force will provide me with another pair should I ever have the need.

The point is, be careful that you do not invest what you do have with an emotion that emanates the limited feeling of "This is all there is, and I had better hold on to this stuff like grim death." For others feel that, and it is hard to expect them to release their wealth liberally to you if you don't hold the same attitude. If you see the supply as infinite, then your emotions are balanced, for you know that there will always be more up ahead. Thus, in receiving and giving, you are free. You can receive without emotion, and you can give in the same way.

What is spiritual abundance? It cannot just be mailing a check to the Ethiopians. It's more. It is that point of mature consciousness whereby you see value and worth in all things. There is a spiritual rivulet of energy that defines all things and because it flows through reality, it underpins it and grants it worth. For you to align to that understanding and live it, trusting in it, is spiritual abundance in my view.

To elevate your consciousness and to practice the *feeling* of flowing abundance, try—for a while, anyway—not saying "thank you" when people give you things. Just take the item and accept it, as the tiger would take its lunch in the forest without so much as an "if you please and would you mind." The idea is to see the coming and going of things as natural and unemotional. You expected it. Then when you give of yourself or of your possessions, you also should not expect anything in return. Just give and move on.

Thus, a balance develops both in your receiving and in your giving. The less resistance you create, the more flow. That, of course, is the key to life. In dropping your resistance, you may seem at first to be more vulnerable, yet eventually that lack of resistance will put you in the flow. Thus, by holding on to nothing, you get everything.

So much for thinking and feeling. Let us turn our attention to action without which your consciousness remains much like two skeletons making love in a biscuit tin—all rattle and wind and no substance.

"To the marketplace." Let us hap upon the affairs of man and declare ourselves in!

Concerted Action in the Marketplace

The basic physical aspects of abundance are your actions in the marketplace of life. The Universal Law cannot mail you a check from the clouds. At some point you will have to get into the marketplace, find other humans, satisfy their needs in some way, and have them transfer a little symbology to your bank account. That's the recognized way.

As you begin to open up to new possibilities and expand yourself, you will have to get "out there" and discover what is really happening in the world. It's pointless to raise your energy and have loads of people attracted to what you are if you haven't got something to sell 'em when they show up.

That means, in basic terms, that you have to have a skill, knowledge, or product. There is nothing else in the world that people want. Of these three broad headings, a skill seems to me to be the least attractive. The problem with it being that you have to roll up each day and do it yourself personally. This can be time-consuming, and eventually time may limit how much you can earn, in total, for offering that skill. However, a skill does have an upside, especially in a world where everyone is mostly useless at what they do. If your skill is offered out of excellence and caring, if that excellence is understood and appreciated by people, then it will be impossible for you to starve. For the competition, wallowing as it does in mediocrity, allows you to stand out from the crowd without any real effort. And as long as you are effective and invest in letting people know who you are and what you do, your future is held in an ironclad guarantee.

Again, we return to the point of your having to invest in yourself. The reason why most people are so pathetic is that they will not take the time to develop and refine their skill. There is such a headlong rush to make it in life, to acquire the accouterments of a fancy lifestyle, that people tumble out and try to merchandise themselves before they have any real experience and while they know little about their chosen field.

Doing so, they sentence themselves to perpetual struggle, for their efforts are mired in the same mediocrity offered by others. I think the old European system whereby people were apprenticed to a master craftsman for seven years had its merits, for although the individual lived on a subsistence level through those years, he or she came out of that experience with pride and a real skill. That talent was honored and recognized by society as being special.

It is important to remember that quality will always survive. If you can perform a function well, you not only have the pleasure of knowing that you're damn good at what you do, but also you will eventually have a niche in the marketplace from which you can never be moved.

To become special, you will have to turn and move against the tide. The masses, drugged by apathy, living a mind-numbing existence and devoid of spirit, demand constant titillation and instant gratification. Thus, as their children become teenagers, it is natural for those children to react in the same way, caring little for excellence and the long term, living instead on a vapid diet of instant returns lacking enduring substance. And why should anyone bother? If it doesn't work for them, then some anonymous body will fix it if things get too bad.

In old China, skills were revered, and although the gardener was socially below the emperor, it was through his ability as a gardener that he redeemed himself and reached his goal in life. From the old Taoist philosophy, there developed in Japan, *Zen,* in which action or order arises from one's attunement with the flow of things. A set of circumstances or even a skill has within it a perfection just for its very sake, and the end product of that perfection is honored for assisting in the overall balance of things. Thus, a Zen master potter is revered, for he creates beauty. And that beauty, because it is perfect, assists people to see the God-force in all things. So his work is eternal and Godlike—it has spirit and meaning. It has worth that everyone recognizes, for in the shape and quality of his pots rests a material evidence of the immortality and infinity of all things.

But for most people, imbuing their every act with excellence is just an intellectual concept. That excellence has to be acquired over a period of time. Most will not invest the time and effort involved, for they don't see that the product of their skills has an intrinsic merit that goes beyond what it can be sold for. There is a spiritual godliness that drifts naturally through the affairs of man, but it is visible *only* if actions are undertaken and performed with that godliness in mind.

If you offer a skill in the marketplace of life, and that skill is lifeless and lacking, then in performing that skill day to day your whole energy takes on the same rhythmic boredom. Gradually that boredom forces you to seek elsewhere, and you will chop and change constantly, never attaining a proper skill at any one thing. It is better, therefore, that you instill a spiritual view in your work and see that your actions have a quality that provides spiritual growth as well as financial return. In this way, your actions become holy and have meaning. How long a thing takes is irrelevant, provided an overall balance is maintained. It is difficult for people to see a specialness in what, for the most part, seems dreary and mundane. Yet, is the God-force not in the people? And if so, then where is the evidence of that God-force if not in the actions and productions of those people?

If a skill or craft is not your line, then perhaps you have knowledge that you can offer. We live in the information age. There are billions of people crying out to know how to do it. So if you know how it's done or where it is, or what to do with it when they get it, you can share that information with others.

What is nice about knowledge is that it can be imparted in many ways. Most of those ways don't involve you after the initial production period, especially now that we are so sophisticated in our dispatch and retrieval methods. Knowledge can be imparted in a hundred ways: TV, audio tapes, books, manuals, floppy disks, compact disks, microfilm, seminars, and, or course, the personal approach. Knowledge is incredibly valuable. Yet, often people miss the point for they can't imagine others paying them for a thought-form. But knowledge is a commodity, and you can sell it. "I know how to do this, pay me, and I'll show you." "I know where the last loaf of bread in New York is, give me a grand, and I'll tell you."

Now, if you don't have information that anyone wants, then you are forced to invest in the acquisition of it. Some people believe in the overriding power of the educational system and feel that without a college degree one isn't likely to make it in life. The problem is, that for the most part, what they teach in college nobody wants. Plus, everyone else got taught the same stuff when they were in college, so everybody knows it. I could see how a college degree would help if you wanted to help others get degrees they can't use. And I can see how a college degree might help if you were hoping to do brain surgery and stuff. But probably half of all the degrees they dish out won't get you a job frying hamburgers. So you've got to decide if you want to mess with spending three to five years studying something that maybe no one will buy.

I met a man once who got a grant to study some kind of beetle in South America. I asked him what he hoped to achieve, as I felt that the demand for that kind of work was not extensive. He told me that he was doing the research for the research's sake and nothing more. I told him that if he'd been clever enough to get a bunch of idiots to give him a grant to study some dumb beetle, then he was clever enough to go out and make a pile of cash. So what was the point of this beetle stuff? In the end, I got it. The reason this man was studying a beetle that no one wanted was so he could avoid having to enter the marketplace of life for a few more years. The beetle developed meaning, not because anyone really cared what the hell the beetle did or didn't do, but because he needed it. No doubt he trotted off up a palm tree somewhere and counted beetles until the free money ran out. But what a waste.

Of course, you don't have to have a degree to be rich. You just have to have ideas. Maybe having a degree sets you back, for it stuffs you into tick-tock, and perhaps that stifles your creative mind. But the fact is that many millionaires have few educational qualifications of any kind at all. However, they still have knowledge. The difference is, they have knowledge they can sell, and others have the "common knowledge" of tick-tock, which isn't worth as much, if anything at all.

The point about knowledge is that if you can sell the knowledge in some kind of educational or informative format, you can use it to place you in a profit-making situation, or you can sell the end product. For example, by taking time to inform yourself about the various conditions of the marketplace, you will soon discover price differences that exist from place to place. That information is valuable to you, for you can then busy yourself moving stuff to places where people want it, at prices they want to pay. But it always comes back to, what do you know that others don't, or who do you know?

The other thing that strikes me about knowledge is that you

don't necessarily have to come up with some earth-shattering idea to get you going in the knowledge business. You can just review what is already known and then come up with a new package or some fresh slant, and people will respond. In fact, when you're selling knowledge, you don't actually want to be too far away from the run-of-the-mill, for if you are too way out, people don't understand what the hell it is that you're trying to sell them.

Now if knowledge is not your game, perhaps you are a merchant at heart. Then product is the way to go. Of course the fun of selling products is that there is no real limit to how many you can sell. Once you have a successful product in the market, you just produce it over and over and sell it to more and more people. What is nice about that is that you don't get paid according to how much work you do, but rather you earn through markup. And so you enter into an energy for which there is no limit.

The trick to buying and selling products is that you've got to choose something that you're interested in. Pick things that you truly love, for if you find yourself selling something that you have no interest in, sooner or later your motivation begins to fade. The negativity and struggle of the marketplace will begin to get you down, and eventually you won't sell enough of the item to grant you a decent living. Everything will drift into an endless spiral of "lousy and getting lousier."

So, if you sell plastic toilet seats that play the theme of *The Bridge Over the River Kwai* when the customer sits down, you have to love that sound. As soon as you hear the whistling of the "Colonel Bogey March," your whole aura has to glitter with awe and inspiration so that you're wandering around the showroom like Tinkerbell. Otherwise, the seats become humdrum, and the selling of them becomes just a way of earning a living, the drabness of which will rot your brain.

Of course, toilet seats may not be your chosen field, but that is irrelevant. Someone will do it and do it well. Let me tell you about a certain English gent called Thomas Crapper. Ol' Tom lived some time in the last century. In the mid-1850s, old Mr. Crapper manufactured and distributed toilet bowls (known as water closets in those days), which became all the rage in Victorian England. So much so that the shortened version of Tom's last name became slang for bowel movement. Thomas Crapper had stamped his name upon a fledgling industry so much so that his product and his name became generic. Over a hundred years later, the company that bears his name still trades in the same business, providing a range of toilet fixtures for discerning customers worldwide. For every old sock there is a shoe. All you have to do is find a niche for yourself, put a touch of class into your efforts, and away you go.

By loving your product, you impart a bit of yourself to every item you offer. It takes on a life of its own that is "you" shaped. When people buy it, they buy a part of you. It is as if in carrying away that item, they carry with them a memento or feeling that they treasure. Have you ever wondered why holiday souvenirs sell so well even though they're so cheap and shoddy? It's because the souvenir is imbued by the customer with the emotional memories of a happy time. So instead of being this grotesque plastic bull standing in an ashtray, it becomes a symbol of positive, carefree days—a holiday romance, perhaps. Now you can do the plastic bull routine on anything you've got, you just have to mentally project yourself into it. This can be a conscious meditation type of thing or an unconscious energy that you give your product because you care for it and love it.

I know a sleazy character of dubious repute who runs a health food store in California. If you are in tune when you walk into his store, he'll be out. But aside from that, I learned two very interesting merchandising features from this fellow. In addition, meeting this man reminded me of one of those important facts of life—namely, that even though someone may be two-thirds of four-fifths revolting, everyone has redeeming features and everyone teaches us something. If nothing else, they offer you a lesson that helps you recognize and remember what types of energy make you throw up!

Anyway, what is interesting about his store is that the music played in the shop is classical rather than New Age, and it is played very, very loud. This tweaks your attention as you walk in, for most New Age stores play that alkaline tinkle, tinkle music that sounds like three dogs piddling in a tin. In contrast, his rousing music has a way of sparking you up, calling you to action, which helps sales. Further, I noticed that every so often he would go around and touch each and every item in the place. He especially cared to touch, and turn, all items that were on sale or with which he was stuck. He explained that within a few days of his touching an item and caring for it, he invariably sold it. By injecting your products with your energy, you change them.

Years ago, traveling in the western United States, I came upon a shop that sold household ornaments—porcelain figures, stained glass, potpourri, that kind of stuff. What was interesting about this operation was that the shop was so well laid out. It had such a magical atmosphere that everyone wanted to go into it just to look around. So the owner charged people just to enter the store.

What a fascinating idea, and very metaphysical! If you can get a buck, say, from everyone who enters your store, you then have no emotion about whether you sell your products or not, for you can make $30,000 a month and sell nothing. In fact, everything you have in the store could be nailed down; why would you care? Once you have no emotion about selling or not selling, you detach. As your feelings detach, that creates an energy vacuum around you that naturally pulls people in. And because you are not involved mentally in the selling or not selling of things, the customer is more relaxed. He or she can savor the magic of your store without pressure. Thus, the customer is captivated by the energy of the place and actually buys twice as much, whether he or she wants the item or not. So you sell the magic, not the item.

I went back to that store many times, mainly to understand the system. I noticed that many of the customers were holiday makers. They would pay their entrance fee and wander in, having no particular purpose in mind. Doing so, they would enter into a kind of meditational rapture that was created by the perfume, the music, and the fairylike atmosphere of the place. The items on offer were incredibly unusual. They were definitely not the kinds of thing that would make you get up in the morning and say, "We need a two-foot-high porcelain egg, or our life won't work." Yet there you are, walking out of the store hauling a $600 ceramic egg back to Detroit without even knowing why you got it. And your husband says, "What the hell do we need this egg for?" You reply, "I don't know. It was the magic of the place that got me. I wanted to carry some of that back home with me. So I bought this egg." And your ol' man shrugs and thinks, We've been goosed!

I never met the owner of that store, but there were two things I knew about him. First, he was a living master in the subtle art of selling the sizzle not the steak. Second, he was an expert in his chosen field. He knew his product.

The point to remember about selling things is that, as well as creating atmosphere and excitement around your products, you've got to know what you're selling. And you have to know the business. It is vital to invest in becoming an expert in your chosen-product field. People need information in order to make buying decisions, and the more information you can offer, especially if you can offer that information in an impartial way, the more people will respond. Trust develops, and they come back time and again.

Remember that as a merchant selling a manufactured good or some type of special service, you will always be a little despised and distrusted. This is because merchants have always been looked down upon as profiteering tricksters. Yet if you think about it, you could get by without most of the skills, and you could certainly get by without most of the knowledge if you had to, but let the world try to manage without the products. Three weeks without gas, beer, lightbulbs, or whatever, and the whole place would unravel pronto. Personally, I think the merchant's life is an honorable one. I can see a goodness in working to provide mankind with the things it needs.

The fact that salesmen and merchants are looked down upon is a throwback to the olden days. The aristocracy felt that it was beneath them to have to trade or do work. The intelligentsia and the clergy were happy to rest within the ruminations of the mind, so that left the merchants to provide the people. Entrepreneurs were considered social outcasts, and only one rung up the ladder from the peasantry who were the lowest of the low. Eventually, the aristocracy ran out of money, the intelligentsia was above making any, and the clergy were sustained by maneuvering the people so they had little or no need to produce anything in particular. One day, everyone looked up to realize that the merchants owned the world.

That won them little respect but lots of freedom, for now they had the clout to buy themselves out of the manipulations and restrictions of life. I like merchants, especially ones who know what they are doing—ones who serve by being experts in their field. The very fact that they involve themselves in aspects of life in which I have no interest allows me to concentrate on things that do interest me.

Personally, hardware stores make me queasy. There is something about those little green boxes and those oily little pieces of paper that I've never been able to relate to. Perhaps my lack of dexterity is the issue here, for I have the mechanical aptitude of a tadpole. I never know what I'm doing when I'm in one of those stores, which creates a feeling of helplessness. You go in and say, "Listen, I need this thing, to stick up a diddly in my bathroom," and the assistant says, "Well, do you want the multiswivel toggle flange with the reverse thread, or the right-hand thread..." and you don't know the answer to that stuff. Isn't it a joy when you meet someone who works in the store and who knows all about diddlies and flanges, and he tells you what you need to know and helps you choose the right one? You feel reassured. The fact that you are manually spastic, that you need a run-up just to knock a nail in a wall, slips from your memory, and you imagine yourself to be one of the pyramid builders of yesteryear.

💰 DOLLAR-DANCE CONCEPT 10 💰

*"In order to successfully serve people, you have to psychologically get **underneath** them, which means that while you are serving them, you have to subjugate your ego to their needs (long enough to take their money, anyway)."*

The trick of course—whether you are selling a skill, knowledge, a product, or even a combination of all three—is quality and service. There is little to say about quality except, put it in there—lots of it. People buy it over and over.

Now here's the trick to service. It's subtle, but if you learn it and learn it well, it will stand you in good stead for many a profitable year to come. First, most people haven't a clue about how to serve, for being a servant is not fashionable nowadays. Everyone wants to exert their personality and independence. So, you go into a restaurant, and the waitress comes over, and instead of her concentrating on your every wish and whim, she begins by talking about herself. "Hi, I'm Maisy. I've got to tell ya, I've just finished a course in transcendental meditation. I can't tell ya how much that has helped me with my PMS. My orgasms are all straightened out at last. Top of that, my boyfriend is taking me to Maui in a week or two. Have you ever been to Maui?" And you're sitting there thinking, What am I, a brick wall, a psychiatrist, a bloody travel brochure? I only came in for two eggs and a slice of toast. What's all this PMS and orgasms in Maui stuff?

The point here is that in order to serve people, you have to psychologically get *underneath* them. This does not mean that you are less than those you serve; it just means that while you are serving them, you have to subjugate your ego and your personality to their needs. That is difficult for most people because they need to feel that they are *above* the customer, or at the very least, *equal* to the customer.

But who is above or below, who is more clever or more rich, is irrelevant to the transaction. By getting underneath, keeping silent and concentrating on the customer's needs, you give of yourself. The customer feels that transfer of energy and responds. Learning to serve is one of the great money-making tricks in life. You subjugate your anxiety, your anguish, and your needs in favor of the customer's—long enough to do the deal. In serving there is the pleasure of doing things well. You learn humility and make loads of money.

I was in a fancy hotel in Washington, D.C., waiting to give a seminar. I ordered a Perrier from the waiter, and by chance he said to me, "What is the secret to getting tips? Some days I do fairly well, and other days I flop." I told the lad about subjugating his ego. He got it, but not totally. So he asked me to give him an example of what I meant. I said to him, "Imagine a man and his wife coming into your bar. Why are they here? First and foremost, life scares people. Most wander around in various states of unholy terror all of the time. Your customer enters this tranquil and elegant bar for a respite from that terror. He needs to get away, to relax, to have a stable, settled moment in which to refresh himself before heading back into the battle of things.

"As he enters, approach him immediately. Say nothing, other than, 'Good morning, sir. How can I help you?' When he orders, listen. Speak only about his needs, unless spoken to. Let's say your customer wants a vodka and tonic, Ask him, 'Would you like ice, sir? A twist of lemon perhaps, an extra napkin, a bowl of nuts? What can I do for you? Can I get you an extra cushion? Would you like the morning paper? What would your lady like? Tomato juice, orange juice, a list of the local hairdressers? Can I take your canary for a walk while you are sitting here?' In other words, the waiter has to come from a place of concentration, subjugation, and complete, limitless service. Nothing is too much trouble. The customer is always right, even when he is wrong. There is no limit to what you will do to serve while that person is in your bar and in your care."

The young lad got the message, and I left to give my seminar. Four hours later, I returned. The same waiter come over to me beaming—glowing with excitement he was. "Fantastic!" he said. "I did what you said. I concentrated on getting underneath my customers. I can hardly believe it! Until now my record for a four-hour shift was $42 in tips. This shift I made $162. One man alone tipped me 40 bucks!"

To serve is honorable. But it is also crafty. There is the hard way in life, where you feel unsure of yourself so you have to project a seeking of people's affection and approval. And then there is the easy way. You feel good about yourself. You can serve in silence without it affecting your self-image. You are proud to serve and to do a good job. You need no acknowledgment, for you have granted that acknowledgment to yourself in advance, in silence. You want nothing for yourself. And in wanting nothing other than to serve your customer, you get everything and more. Life is simple. Mostly it's a matter of going in the opposite direction of the average twit. Nothing more.

Years ago I had a partner named David. We worked as jobbers in the clothing industry. Our function was to go around to factories and buy up seconds, slightly irregular clothing, end-of-line garments, and so forth. The name of that game is to give the factory as little as possible for the items so that no matter how horrible the clothing is, you can at least make a profit on some of it and then junk the rest at break even or better.

We walked into this fellow's office one day, and I started talking about the deal. As I did so, David, who was a large man—over 200 pounds—lay down on the floor in front of the man's desk. I tried to take no notice, but David's huge frame, lying there like Moby Dick, was hard to ignore. A few moments later, I joined him on the carpet. Somehow it seemed the right thing to do. We both negotiated from ground zero, more or less under the factory owner's desk. We did the deal and hauled out to the parking lot. Once there, I asked David what the hell was going on, and he explained to me that the subtle art of negotiating is to get underneath the seller and sustain a nonthreatening position. You can't get uptight about two loonies who are lying on your carpet. Ironically, we did a hell of a deal that day. The factory had a whole pile of jeans with crooked seams. The outside seam of those jeans started at the waist and gradually curved around the knee to finish up as an additional inside seam that defied any rational explanation. We bought the job lot, chopped off the offending lower legs, and sold the finished items as denim shorts. Bingo! There's no limit to the creative mind.

8

Originality: The Recipe for Easy Money

A s you think in terms of what you are going to sell 'em, I think we ought to discuss originality for a moment, for it is your recipe for easy money. Very little out there is original, yet if people find something truly unusual—providing it works okay— they flock to be a part of it. Look at Disneyland. There are theme parks all over the world, but Disneyland stands out. People travel thousands of miles just to spend a few hours there.

Have you ever noticed that many things are not built for the convenience of the user? It seems that often people's needs are irrelevant to the manufacturer's design decisions. For example, how often have you seen a bath faucet that you can operate with your feet? It stands to reason that you are not going to want to get out of a warm bath to reach the other end to turn off the tap. Yet somehow, almost every bath in the world has a nobbly little handle that's awkward to operate and miles away. It's hard enough to turn the knob with a soapy hand, but with your feet, forget it. A contortionist would have trouble. The first guy who comes up with a foot-operated bath faucet will be an instant millionaire.

When I look at things that don't work too well, it excites me.

I see the glimmer of easy money. Over the last few years, I have flown around a lot. The equivalent of 83 times 'round the world. I have noticed that airlines are packed with examples of things that don't emotionally work for the customer.

The point about flying is that the customer doesn't give a damn whom he or she flies with, providing they get there. The problem is that many of the airlines nowadays are tossing the customers out at sea or banging them into the tarmac. PR-wise this goes down like a brick balloon. When I get on a plane that's oily and dirty, it creates instant concern. For my mind naturally wonders if all the bits and bobs are working. Continental Airlines in the U.S. is a good example of this. For some reason that I don't understand, they oil their aircraft before each day's commerce. With so much oil external to the craft, it naturally makes one wonder if there is any in the engine. What would it take to wash those planes once a week? Not much. How many customers do the airlines lose because folk take poorly to flying in a garbage bag?

Another thing I noticed about Continental Airlines is that they have the word CACA stamped on their silverware. No doubt the logo stands for something logical like "Continental Airlines Catering Administration" or whatever. However, *caca* to most people means "shit." I'd love to meet the genius at Continental who's getting $100,000 a year to print *caca* on the spoons!

Anyway, once comfortably crammed into your seat, the next performance is the hostess's safety routine. The sight of that young lady waving that plastic card rattles me enormously. You know that she's doing her very best, but as she waves her arms about, pointing to the doors and exits, you look at the 300-pound passenger who's jamming the aisle, and you know you'll never make it. Next, on goes the yellow life jacket, which serves to remind you of some rotten possibilities. But take heart, there's a whistle on the jacket, they tell you. Now, if you're bobbing about in the dark 600 miles east of Fiji, you can at least whistle some happy little tune to cheer you up.

As the hostess up front continues her pantomime, you casually look down at your feet at the little screw that bolts the seats in front of you to the floor. The screw is about the size of the nail on your little finger. What is particularly disturbing about that little screw is, first, its size; and second, the realization that an exact replica of that same screw is all that is holding *your* seat to the floor.

Meanwhile the young lady up front is ceremoniously clicking the belt buckle in and out, and you naturally wonder, in the event of the plane hitting something unusual, what earthly good would the belt do you. Next time you fly, take a look at that screw. Perhaps you could get a piece of paper and a pencil and make a rubbing of it. When home, you'll notice that the screw is about the same size as the one that holds the fridge door on, and your fridge is unlikely to be hurtling around at 400 miles an hour!

In the event of an emergency, the airline tells you to take off your shoes, bend over, and grab your ankles. The logic of that completely escapes me. If you're going to be flying through the cabin with a seat strapped to your backside, the last thing you are going to want to do is to look silly. I finally concluded that the reason they want you hurtlin' about with your head between your knees is that it is a handy position for kissing your arse goodbye. What would it take to put a decent screw on the floor? Pennies. Are they going to do it? Probably not.

It is hard to say to someone, "Be original." It's like saying, "Be a great singer." Either they can sing or they can't. Yet there are ways of thinking through the presentation of your service, or even the presentation of yourself, that is fresh and unusual so that it stimulates people's attention. Often that is only a matter of thinking through what others might want and trying your best to provide that. Just a slight touch is all it takes.

For example, certain restaurants nowadays pack out the room with plants and flowers. I don't mean the odd arrangement here and there. They make the flowers a part of the atmosphere. There are literally hundreds of hanging baskets, trees, and so forth all over the joint. I've never gone into that type of restaurant when it has not been busy. People like plants and flowers. The energy they give off is fresh and clean and rejuvenating, which is why they go into a restaurant in the first place.

Sometimes your originality can be just to *not* do what all the others do. For example, how many times have you been to a restaurant where the waiters or waitresses look as if they haven't washed for a month or two? You take one look at those characters, and their demeanor automatically sets up a tension within you. Looking down at your soup spoon you think, *Lick this and die.* Perhaps your originality could be that everything in your restaurant is absolutely spotless all of the time.

Personally, I like things that are a bit bizarre. I love to set up scenarios that no one understands. In fact, using bizarre images is often good merchandising for people's imagination because their memory is stimulated. The Heineken beer campaign that has run in Europe for many years is one of the most successful ever devised. The caption reads, "Heineken's refreshes the parts that other beer cannot reach." The graphic is usually some bizarre scene of a guy with a flowering bush coming out of his head. No one has a clue as to what the ads mean, but everyone remembers them.

In western Canada, there is a small brewery that makes a beer called Kokanee. In their TV commercials, they have a dog called Brew. The dog is owned by friends of mine. In the ad, the dog catches a taxi to the liquor store and then heads over hill and dale to bring a six-pack of Kokanee beer back to his TV owner, who is camped in the forest. The image is emotive and funny. In less than a year, Kokanee went from being an obscure little brewery to being a household name in Canada.

Originality allows you to stand out from the crowd. In America, the citizens are bombarded by 600 or more advertising messages per day. What you offer could be fantastic, but how will you position it out and away from the pack? A bit of originality at the front end saves you fortunes later on. It's an expensive drag to try to haul a dull product into the minds of the public.

I have this idea for a restaurant in which there would be a large pit just inside the front door. In the pit I'd toss a few alligators. Big ones, with large teeth and open mouths. Then I'd build a bridge over the pit. All my customers would have to cross it in order to get to the tables. I'd make the bridge a little rickety. Not too much so, but just enough to get people thinking. Next I'd hire a fellow from the zoo to figure out how high an alligator can jump on its best shot. I'd pitch my bridge a few inches higher than the best the 'gators could hope for.

People would flock from miles around just to get over the alligator pit. As they'd come in, they'd ask, "Isn't it dangerous?" "Yeah, we lose a few," I'd say, "but the rest are real hungry when they get to the other side." What would it cost to buy a few alligators? A few grand, perhaps. Maybe you could have the alligator pit running throughout the restaurant. The customers would love to toss their bread rolls into the pit and watch them disappear in one gulp.

Subliminally the idea is terrific. What better symbol for eating than an alligator with its jaw open, chomping on stuff inches from your leg? People would come to eat there even if the food were lousy, just for the action. There's something interesting going on. You could charge what you liked.

Every so often you could fake it a little and throw a dummy in the water without anyone knowing. The commotion would catch people's attention and quicken their adrenals, increasing their appetite. "What's happening?" they'd ask. "Oh, nothing much. We've just lost the wine waiter. That's the third this month." When you think of all the money people spend decorating restaurants! And what you get is all chrome and glass and boring for the most part. All you have to do is hang half a dozen boa constrictors off the fans, and away you go.

Things have to be interesting in order to get people's attention. They want to learn something; they want to be challenged in some way, or just involved. Engage people whenever you can have them be a part of the act, so to speak. They love it. If you own a photocopying store, you're thinking, *How do I make photocopying original and interesting?* There is always a way. Stick one of your old photocopiers on the ceiling. When people come in and want a photocopy, point upwards and let them figure it out for a moment or two. When they ask the obvious question—"Why is the machine on the ceiling?" tell them you figured out that you were paying rent for the ceiling so to make the business more cost-effective you stuck the machine up there. "How many copies would you like, sir?"

Personally, I think if things are lighthearted and amusing, people respond. Now you can't have the bank manager dressed up in a clown's outfit, for in the area of finances people are really serious. It's too much of a survival issue to make fun of. Old man Rockefeller once said, "Making money is serious business." He must have known; he had more money than God. So in dealing with tick-tock on the subject of money, you've got to be straight. But everything else can have a sense of the loony to it.

I have this idea for a doctor's office. Going to a doctor's surgery is no picnic. The best part is leaving. There is nothing like the exhilaration of crossing the car park on the way out, kicking your heels, knowing that you aren't going to croak it for a while yet, anyway. All the rest of the experience is a complete drag, a tension. How do you make it fun? You put a little theater into it.

The patient would come in and lie on the couch. The doctor would examine the patient. Near the couch would be a little mouse running 'round on a wheel. On each rung on the wheel would be written a kind of drug or treatment. Once the doctor had finished his examination, he'd say to the mouse, "What do you think?" The mouse sets off, trotting round the wheel, and wherever it stops the doctor reads off the prescription. There's the mouse, wobbling around on the wheel after its little run, and the doctor leans over and says to the patient, "Ah, yes, it says here, what you really need is a hundred milligrams of toxy-poxy-tetra-cycline."

Now this would engage the client's interest. "How does the mouse know where to stop?" asks the patient. "Oh, he's highly qualified." says the doctor. "Amazing," says the patient, "I've never seen it done that way." Of course the patient lying down on the couch would not be able to read each rung of the wheel as it hurtled past, so the doctor could fake it to make sure the patient got the right stuff. But it would be great. Eventually, the mouse would become famous. People in perfect health would roll up for an examination at the doc's, just to see the mouse operate its routine.

Anyway, if you don't like that idea I've got another. What about an insurance salesman who goes door-to-door on an elephant? People like their insurance companies to be rock solid. What's more rock solid than a two-ton elephant?

In the end it all comes down to enthusiasm. Your creativity is basically your expression of God-force. There is nothing more marvelous than doing something you love to do and getting paid for it. It ceases to become work, money, and effort; and it becomes fun, your expression of the joy of life. My idea has always been to make everything you do into a game. Now people might say that this is childlike. But what do you care as long as you can count to a million and are having fun? In a world where everyone is so bloody serious, we need a few confident, light-hearted loonies to keep things moving along.

Anyway, when a person is really serious about life, what he or she is usually saying is, "I can't cope. It's all too overwhelming." One feels insecure. You can see this in offices where some immature little boy is placed in the position of manager. The uptight twit starts making life a misery for everyone because he feels unsure of himself. If you work for one of those cardboard cutouts, roll into work tomorrow with a large lemon meringue pie. Say, "Good morning, sir," in your most serious tone. Then smash the idiot in the mouth with the pie. Of course, that may wind up being your last creative effort for the firm, but it's better that you go somewhere else and live and work with people who are happy and alive, rather than putting your efforts into supporting an acid bath.

9

The Force of
Your Will Projected

The quality of your "concerted action in the marketplace" is really dominated by the force, or lack thereof, of your intention. Most people think that intention just means saying, "I'll do my best." When people say that to me, I run a mile. "I'll do my best," is the mind's way of saying, "I'll trot out there and play around doing busy work for an hour or two, and when the project doesn't succeed or realize its full potential, I'll be okay because I have my excuse already pinned on the wall."

Your mind is your best friend, but it's also an enemy. Not only because it has a vested interest in limiting what you believe you can do, but also because it has a way of selling you short. Isn't it interesting that whenever a group of people set out to develop a project, that project usually falls short of everyone's expectations? In real life, things never quite pan out the way one thinks they ought to. Why is that? Because the ego-personality is happy to spend four hours in a meeting talking about building apartments on the beach, but it isn't at all happy spending eight hours actually hauling cement or delivering sales pitches to prospective buyers. Imagination and "concerted action" live in different neighborhoods.

So as you set out with your battle plan, be careful to analyze beforehand what your intention is. If it is wishy-washy, the realities of life will have a way of making sure your project doesn't work. Your intention has to be at the forefront of your thinking and has to be followed by timely action, which is appropriate to deliver that intention.

You see, you can wander out into the lot and say to yourself, *I hope I'll sell a couple of cars today.* Or, you can arrive at work 15 minutes early, organize your desk, get your brochures and order forms ready, sharpen your pencil, and say to yourself, *I expect to sell six cars or more. Nothing less is acceptable.* The other salesmen might say that six cars a day is impossible, for it takes an average of two hours to sell a car. So the most you might hope for is, say, four cars a day, not six. But they are coming from a place of selling one car to one person, for that is what is normal for them, and you are coming from intention, which has no opinion of how many cars you might sell to whom or how long it might take. It just says six cars or more!

So you sell two cars by lunchtime, and then nothing happens for three hours. Then a fellow wanders in and asks, "How much is that Rolls Royce?" You say, "One hundred twenty thousand dollars and change, sir." He says, "I'll take four. One pink, one blue, and two green."

So you see there is tick-tock, and then there is intention. In tick-tock, any old excuse is fine as long as you don't have to deliver. Intention says, no limit here. Nothing can stop me. I feel it. I see it in my mind's eye. I have focused *will* as the laser beam of my intent. I am involved. I persist. Nothing is too much trouble. My intention has to be delivered, for I insist on it. I won't quit until it is. Of course on some days, circumstances go against you. In spite of your readiness and high intention, it pelts down rain all day, and you don't sell your six cars. However, you were ready and open. If anyone had walked into the showroom with even half an inclination, they would have gone out with one of your cars. And that is all that matters, for when the force of your *will* is honed and you are consistent in your actions, life eventually has to deliver to you what it is that you want.

💰 DOLLAR-DANCE CONCEPT 11 💰

"On your quest, think of the symbology of the woodpecker. Each peck does not amount to much, but eventually the whole bloody tree comes down."

Persistence and patience are the keys to intention. But for that to work, you have to be able to focus and concentrate on the target. Most people quit before the final payout, which is sad, but that's life. I was in a silver mine where the old miners had dug and dug for years and found only a trickle of silver here and there. When they finally quit digging they were just 12 feet from a multimillion-dollar mother lode. The modern owner of the mine was happy with that. He moved the diggings over—a couple of yards or so—and bingo!

I have always been keen on the philosophy of the ancient Mongols. What we learned from those guys, like it or not, is intention. When the lads set out to get somewhere, they arrived. They didn't so much conquer the land, they rolled it up and took it with them! The Mongols were brilliant organizers. In fact, their word *orda* gave rise to our word *order*. What we learn from them is their ability to stick to the project, no matter what. They could ride in anguish and pain. Conditions were irrelevant to them. The intent was the only thing that mattered.

So often we expect things in life to be cozy and guaranteed. We demand that things happen in a certain format or in a predetermined way, otherwise we deem them to have failed. You can have all the intention in the world, but sometimes things arrive from a different direction. What you are looking to do within intent is to focus on the target and never let go, no matter how long it takes. The great fortunes of the world were not built overnight. Things take time, and you have to be able to wait. If you are no good at waiting, start learning how. Being able to out-wait the opposition is another of the great secrets to life. It is very Taoist. And it is also very crafty. When you know that all the world is in a rush, all you have to do is hold the other view.

I like the symbology of the woodpecker. Each peck does not amount to much, but eventually the whole bloody tree comes down. As you focus on your target, take *woodpecker* with you. It will become a good friend. By holding the overall plan in your mind and concentrating on the pecking, you will eventually get what you want. When you think about it, what's the rush? If you are balanced, there is none. If you are not balanced, the rush, in itself, will push what you want away from you. One step at a time. Force yourself to pause and take stock, to rebuild and then head out again.

What I learned from the European occultists is that the great-est power available to us humans is our *will* when projected cor-rectly. Now you probably haven't thought much in terms of the power of your *will*. But it is this same power that the ancient magi-cians used to create supernatural events in their lives. The differ-ence between *will* and intention is that for many people, intention is just a mental act—a kind of wishful thinking—whereas the force of *will* projected from your consciousness contains not only your thoughts and desires, but also the enthusiasm of your own Life-force. Your *will*, projected correctly, will contain that vital ingredient, your *spirit*—the very essence of what you are.

The force of that *spirit*, clearly defined, will deliver to you the focus of your *will*, by virtue of the fact that the clarity of its concentration is honed to such an uncluttered purity that it cuts right through reality and fires the full weight of its power upon any target. Remember that your consciousness is contained in a sea of consciousness, which is basically all the energy and thought-forms of the world around you. For the most part, the energy of people around you will be weak and ill-defined. What little power they have is often undermined by emotion.

In that pea soup of mumbling and grumbling, along comes the magician: powerful, clear, and uncluttered by yearnings or fanciful rambles of the imagination. Detached as he is from the emotions of humanity, he stands on a launch platform that is already a rung or two higher than the crowd. From there he fires his *will* into the circumstances of life, knowing that his power is unstoppable.

How could the Universal Law of life deny this man? It can't. His power is too great. His *will* is uncluttered by any thought of deserving, of good and bad, of having or not having. It is focused solely on what he wants. His desire is not delivered because of any higher selection process; rather, it comes to him solely through the force of his demand. It is because he wants it, because that thought is laced in his *will*, empowered by the very spirit of his being, that it cannot be denied him.

When first confronted by this idea, I had a natural reaction against the aggression needed to reach that certain level of intent. It seemed to me that somehow it was "wrong" to harness one's power in occult terms, to force life to hand over one's every wish and whim. But gradually I got used to the idea and developed a theory of morality around my particular method. Soon I realized that what was important to me were my achievements—the things that I knew I had to complete in this lifetime. How I got those things, providing I did not infringe on others, was irrelevant.

The points to consider are: What do you want, and how much energy are you prepared to exert to get what you want? If the level of enthusiasm you are willing to commit to your quest is not great, then obviously you don't want what you think you do, or at best your quest is not that important to you. But if some aspect is very, very special to you, it becomes sacred by virtue of its integrity. Then the level of your commitment to that ideal is vital, for you know that the whole reason for your life is contained and centered in that one quest or achievement.

If this is so, you are required by its very sacredness to exert every fiber of your being, through physical effort, mental acuity, or occult power, to deliver the focus of your intent. Somewhere in your life there will be an overriding theme to your quest— some part of your desire that cannot be denied without a terrible cost to the very essence of what you are. Are you going to ignore it, or do you have the courage of your commitment and the confidence to demand that life, humanity, or circumstances give you what you want, with no other excuse, reason, or apology other than that you demand it?

If the level of your intention is thus, you have gripped the idea of the force of *will*. If, however, your commitment is less than powerful, life will not give you what you want, for it has no concern for your well-being; neither does it have a knowledge of your wants. The only way is for you to indicate your desire, hold it in the forefront of your thoughts, and aggressively demand— better still, *insist*—that life deliver.

Some might say that this is not spiritual, that it feels like ripping a plaque off a museum wall. Perhaps in certain circumstances that is true. But does it follow that, while you may demand certain things of life, you should also fail to be a kind and loving person? No, it does not. All it says is that in one or two areas of your life you will not compromise. Rather, it seems to me that your life would lack spiritual definition if, while realizing that some particular aspect of your quest was vital, you nevertheless failed to exert the full pressure of your intent in seeking that vital aspect. You might look back on your life and see this kind, generous, and loving person who was totally wimpy, however, when asking for his or her needs to be met. You would see that you had indeed learned to love others, but in doing so had allowed the world to walk all over you. You had failed to materialize your dreams because of your self-deprecating attitude. In loving the world, you forgot to love yourself. So half the lesson is learned, and the other half remains to be handled at some later date, perhaps. What a drag.

The constant problem of the force of *will* when projected is the question of what an infringement is. For example, if you were to fire a thought into the mind of another, forcing that person to have sex with you against their will, that would be an infringement, for the manipulation required to achieve your desire is too intense. But what if the power of your *will* (the energy that is collected around you) is so overwhelmingly forceful that it creates in another the overriding urge to be with you, to do absolutely anything to be in your company? When that person approaches you and says, "I will do anything to be with you," you might say, "Fine, but the condition I place in granting your request is that I require you to have sex with me every second Thursday."

That, to me, is not an infringement, for you have the right to demand for yourself whatever is reasonable. The fact that the person in front of you has an overwhelming emotional need to be with you does not mean that you are required to fulfill that need. Neither does it mean that you should have to acquiesce to their wishes without getting something in return. To some, sex every second Thursday would be a small inconvenience compared with the perceived benefit of your allowing them to hang out with you. You will not know until you ask whether or not they would consider your request reasonable. But either way, you have been clear, and you have communicated your terms, and they can decide one way or the other.

As you project the force of your *will* into life, it creates awkward situations for people through its unusual power. For it forces them to evaluate their needs in light of yours. It is natural for people to expect you to share your energy or knowledge or physical self free of charge, and regardless of whether or not it is convenient to you. There is a tendency for us to feel that we have to give constantly. This is not necessarily so, for you are an individual and you, too, have needs.

Yet, when your *will* is clear, strong, and focused, people will tend to bump up against it. It forces them to accept terms they may have not considered before. Perhaps they feel that you ought to hang out with them and spend your time on them free of charge. It is natural for people to expect things from you for nothing, for you have offered it in the past. Why would they pay or trade if they don't have to? Yet when something costs nothing, it usually means that the individual considers it valueless. If, then, hanging out with you is valueless to them, why would you mess with wasting your time on it?

The subtle point here is for you to make sure that your *will* does not force others into actions that offend their morality (even if their morality is a bit silly), or is against their will. As long as you offer them an exit, they are free to choose. And if "sex every second Thursday," is not agreeable to them, they can always refuse or come back with an alternative offer.

What I saw among the European occultists was that for the most part, their magical practices were a lot of *hocus-pocus*. In any method, the proof of the pudding is in the eating, and what I saw were a lot of scruffy little fellows waffling on about the power of their magic, while in reality they didn't have two beans to rub together.

Then, again, from time to time I met a real pro, someone who was wealthy, powerful, and successful. But those characters were very secretive, and it was hard to eke a methodology from them. One day I was a guest at lunch in a fancy restaurant while one of those hairy little characters was entertaining his banker. The occultist ordered a bottle of d'Yquem, which impressed me, because d'Yquem is one of the finest and most expensive white wines in the world. As food was served and the conversation drifted back and forth, I could see that the occultist was messing with the banker's mind. It wasn't long before he flipped the banker with a blanket of energy that contained a ferocious amount of the occultist's power—and all of his *will*.

The flip consisted of a thought-form thrown from the area of the heart over the banker's head, like a blanket. The energy of the thought-form projected thus is gray/blue in color. Its power is defined by the force of one's *will* and the clarity of one's intent. The banker reacted by leaning back from the table and affecting a somewhat disconnected and glazed look in his eye. He lost his concentration and stumbled on his words. He knocked a roll to the floor. It seemed to me that his ability to resist was shot away. In the next two minutes, the hairy little occultist got the banker to commit to an unsecured $300,000 loan. Some months later, by which time I was living in America, the banker called me from Europe, complaining that the hairy little fellow had hightailed with his cash. *A fairly predictable course of events,* I thought.

The strange thing was that although the occultist was crooked in the normal definition of things, he never considered himself a thief. He believed in his power so totally (and he had a right to) that he considered his presence a gift to the world. This was an opinion that was confirmed by almost all who met him. People were delighted to give him their money, and during the period I hung out with him, I saw him unhinge people from their loot to the tune of two and a half million dollars or thereabouts. When parting with their cash, no one seemed to complain. It was only later when he was no longer on the scene and the donors were no longer influenced by his power that everyone had second thoughts.

Crook or not? He was, in a strange way, the most spiritual person I had ever met, for he was truly himself, an individual. Like it or not, he had a methodology, a rule, a code that he lived by. The force of his *will* demanded that life support him on the level to which he had become accustomed, and people responded willingly. He, in turn, was a very generous person. He would give you the shirt off his back, for he considered his supply of abundance limitless. He never for a moment thought that there could be the slightest possibility of his running out.

If he made any mistake, it was that when people went ga-ga over his energy he let them abandon their *will* to his. If he had tempered this somewhat and taken a little here and a little there, no one would have reacted. But the fellow got a bit carried away by his ego, and he began to believe that the Higher Powers had chosen him for some great mission that might well change the destiny of the world.

Naturally, to be burdened with such a karmic obligation would call for massive amounts of other people's money in order to deliver a plan acceptable to the gods. So rather than taking the odd five or ten thousand, he would hit people up for a hundred grand or whatever he could get. One idiot, a rancher from Oregon, handed over $700,000. Well, as the sums of money got bigger, the folk involved got more intense about getting their cash back. For a while, there was a whole little team, along with the Fraud Squad, out looking for the fellow. But our little gnome was much too fast on his feet. With the passage of time, people's anger subsided, and they accepted their losses as "investments," the kind we all line up for as we learn the game of life.

The point is, if your intention is forceful and your *will* is clearly defined, people line up to give you want you want. You have to have confidence in yourself. You have to be able to believe in your own power. If you have the slightest doubt about your worthiness, it takes you immediately from infinite possibilities to a more sparse result.

Imagine the tiger in the forest. Does it wonder if the deer on the path is his? Is there any question of the tiger's worthiness? Being interconnected as all things are, the eternal Tao sustains itself. The little creatures give themselves up to the tiger, as nature gave of itself to sustain the creatures. Perfect balance is maintained.

The mind creates boundaries that are fake and ungodlike. If

you have no real emotion about your possessions, and if you do not cling to life in a desperate way, the Tao emanates from you. Balance is the gift you offer. What, then, if in affirming abundance, you come upon a handbag stuffed with cash? Let us say for argument's sake that the bag contains no identifying marks. You would have to accept that abundance as a natural extension of your energy, or you would be totally negating your alignment to the infinite.

The only thing to watch out for is the danger of going over the top and taking undue advantage of others or getting carried away by the ego. In a world where everyone manipulates or controls everyone else, wouldn't it be nice if you could become a success story without having to resort to the same mucky techniques?

It seems to me that at most we are just custodians of a power. We are not the power itself, and we should remember that. When balanced, the power flows spontaneously and confirms to us the pure spirituality of things. But sometimes the energy within one becomes so powerful and so intense that the individual loses all sight of humble mortality and allows himself to be wafted by ego into thinking that somehow he or she is here to fix the world, to become the oracle of the gods, or whatever.

You can see that nonsense in both the New Age and the major religions. The leaders begin to believe themselves to be divinely selected. There is a secondhand car salesman in America who drifted into the guru business and now has two people to walk beside him, lest any of his followers should accidentally touch him and rob him of a few volts of his newfound divinity. What the followers don't know for the most part is that their car salesman guru is gay. He is not averse to allowing some of the lads to rob him willy-nilly all night long, if need be. Ah! The perfidy of the human mind is endless.

As you concentrate upon yourself and your life, you will soon become much more powerful than 99 percent of those with whom you deal. You should take care to temper your energy and not get carried away by the wealth or the position you find yourself in. If you don't watch carefully, it is likely that sooner or later you will self-destruct. Or worse still, you might achieve your every wish and whim, but look back on your life and see ugliness, see that you achieved your quest in material terms but failed to translate those material benefits into an honorable code of living or spiritual essence. That would be sad. In my view, wealth for its very sake is just an ego trip that is driven by the desires to satiate one's survival worries. In its worst form, money is the ego's way of grasping helplessly for its own immortality. That is why the very rich build monuments. First, it keeps the ego happy; and second, in the bricks and mortar they seek foolishly to perpetuate their own existence.

You have to ask yourself, "Do I sincerely want to be rich?" If the answer is, "Yes," then your next question is, "What do I want the money for?" What will you do if you become loaded? Once these questions are clear in your mind, the target is only a few years away at most. If your quest for wealth is ego-oriented and if at the same time you are trying to develop a spiritual aspect to your life, you will find that your money-making attempts will constantly fail. Your *inner* being will protect you from the possibility of self-destruction, from losing sight of your true goal through the temptation of ego.

If you have no overall spiritual quest, you will probably make money more quickly, but what you achieve will be empty. You should look into your heart and answer those questions, for all the intention and force of *will* in the world will be useless to you if you are not happy, or if your conscious mind is diametrically opposed to your inner quest.

If one asks, "Do you sincerely want to be rich?" most people will answer, "Yes," but not many of those answering in the affirmative will actually mean it. They can imagine wealth and a lush lifestyle, but they don't really believe they can have it, or they don't believe they are worthy, or they are happy for those fantasies to rest solely in the mind and do not actually have the force of intention to go out and get what they want.

If you are going to be very rich, you are going to have to agree to take responsibility and lots of it. You will have to become particularly involved in life. Getting rich is a hands-on process. It involves endless interaction and a certain amount of stress and strain. Is that what you want? It is customary for people to view the rich as living an indolent, carefree life, sipping cocktails at the beach while the chauffeur purrs at the curbside. This may be true for a few, but most have to go out and create their wealth. Once that wealth is achieved, they have to look after it, invest it, and even defend it somewhat. It takes a massive amount of energy, and you have to look and see if you have that level of energy, or if you are prepared to put in what it takes to develop that flair. If you answer, "Yes, I'll do anything," and you sincerely mean it, then you are halfway there. But if you are less than sure, then you should stop and think about it.

Perhaps, if you look deep into yourself, all you need is just a little more abundance so that you can free up your life a little. Perhaps massive wealth would make you very sick. Maybe a bit extra is all you need. If so, you have to ask yourself why you don't have that already. Why are things tight? The answer will lie deep within you somewhere. You can find that answer and fix the problem quickly as long as you are truthful with yourself. Perhaps you have a fear of commitment. Or perhaps you failed to concentrate on things correctly. Or it could be—and this is common—that you have designed a lifestyle that is relatively free, for you have never joined the system. But in denying yourself entry into the system, you have had difficulty in getting that very same system to cough up all that you need. Perhaps you have relegated yourself to eking out an existence in a shantytown on the edge of the city rather than committing yourself to entering the mainstream.

Many are faced with the same problem. Yet sometimes to go

beyond, all one has to do is join. Though "joining" may not be in your heart, by playing the game at least you get what you want from the system. Anyway, if all one needs is a little more, it is good to have identified that intention, and now the task is to work toward the goal.

It is not hard to develop little money machines that crank out cash once you have "intention" and once you are prepared to enter the marketplace and find out what is going on. When you think of it, it doesn't matter how you make that extra cash. You can sell condoms in truck-stop toilets, if need be, as long as you create that little machine and it gives you the balance you seek. Or perhaps you can fix things simply by making what you do so much better, and charging more.

The whole trick to money is balance. Balance at a thousand a month, or balance at a million a month. The great value of that balance is that it underpins the spiritual you and allows the inner beauty and creativity to come out. That is why for most people, money is the one lesson—other than love, perhaps—that we are here to learn.

You should sit down with your loved ones and really discuss your financial needs so that each of you can define what he or she wants and what each one's level of intention is. Then you can tailor your hopes and dreams to suit your intention, and you can see if the level of your projected *will* is going to be strong enough to deliver whatever it is that you want.

If your intention is not really that high, you will have to accept that as fact, and you may have to adjust what you expect from life. Alternately, you can work on your intention through concentration and discipline, to make it stronger. Then once it is strong, the force of your *will* projected into life will guarantee the delivery of your heart's desire.

Of course, sometimes things are so imbalanced financially that it seems almost impossible to get a fresh start. The problem stems from the fact that, nowadays, credit is so easy to obtain.

When I first came to America, it boggled my mind that you could walk into a store and sign for stuff even though the shop didn't know you from Adam. A dollar down, and catch us if you can!

💰 DOLLAR-DANCE CONCEPT 12 💰

"If some aspect (of your life) is very, very special to you, it becomes sacred by virtue of its integrity. Then the level of your commitment to that ideal is vital, for you know that the whole reason for your life is contained and centered in that one quest or achievement."

With so much credit, it is easy to see why people get into trouble. If your debt is out of control, you have a disease—a disease of finances. That, more than anything else, will cause you imbalance. The emotion about owing money is a surefire way of blocking you from opportunity.

Now, if you are in control of your finances, you pay everyone. But if you are way, way out of control, you'll have to lie down in the hospital bed of finances for a little while; otherwise, you will never be healed. You need to rest and to pull back. In an imbalanced state, struggling to pay people is the most stupid way of fixing things. It only encourages them to ask for more, and it rattles you, which is no help to the creditors in the end. Retreat is the only answer.

Of course, it depends on how much you owe. If you're only a little out of control, you can cut back on expenses and pay people off bit by bit. But let's say you are way over the top. The first move is to admit it to yourself. The next is to let your creditors know they ain't getting it anytime soon. Once that is communicated to them clearly, they drop you off the "immediate" list, and you go to the back burner where the emotion is a lot less and you don't have a ferret tugging on your nuts.

Your first reaction might be, "If I don't pay people, won't that destroy my goodwill and credit?" The fact is, mate, your goodwill is already destroyed, and your credit sucks! What do you have to lose? Anyway, you are not going to need credit. After all, credit is only a device to satisfy your cravings when you are not able to satisfy them immediately in cash.

"But what if I lose my credit cards?" So what. You don't need credit if you have money. "Yes, but credit cards are handy when traveling or renting cars." No problem. There are banks that specialize in giving cards to people who have lousy credit. The cards are backed by the customer with a savings account at the bank. "But if I don't pay my debts, people won't like me anymore." Forget it! (Go back to chapter 3 and reread the section on acceptance of self.)

It is better that you declare bankruptcy than try to sustain a position that is untenable. Then, having made a clean sweep of things, you will have to change the error of your ways—no more credit—or, alternatively, small amounts of credit that you can easily handle. If you wipe off the old stuff and then start owing all over again, you have not granted yourself (on an energy level) absolution for the situation because you are engaging in the same old nonsense. Karmically that would be dishonest. But everyone is entitled to make the odd mistake in life and start again. Your creditors are equally as responsible for your debt situation as are you. There are no innocent victims. They made a business decision to give you credit in the hope of a profit, and you failed them. That happens all the time.

Let's say, hypothetically, that you have had a credit card for 20 years, and you have been paying 19 percent interest in addition to the annual fees on that card for that length of time. The credit card company knows exactly what percentage of people default on their bills each year. Let's say it is 2 percent. So the credit company calculates that all their customers will default at least once every 50 years (2% x 50 = 100%). That cost is added into the annual interest and the fees that they charge. So for 20 years you have been paying for your possible default. Why, then, would you want to disappoint them? If you don't default once every 50 years, you're going to start messing around with their mathematics. That would cause a panic!

When you owe money, people harass you, and that can make you feel like a rotten egg. You forget that you are a child of God and immortal and all that good stuff. You tend to get down on yourself and believe all the things your creditors are saying about you. At first it may seem that they are right and that you are powerless. But, in fact, the reverse is the case. The creditors are right, but *they* are powerless. As a debtor, you are in the driver's seat, and you should never forget that.

The emotion lies always with the creditors, and they try to drag the debtor in the same emotional whirlpool. But what if you refuse to be rattled? The fact that you owe someone money and can't pay is no reason for you to be upset. Nothing serious can really happen. If you have assets, the creditor can chase after those assets. Good luck to him! And if you have no assets, you're home free.

In addition, time is usually on your side. Having incurred a loss, the creditor can only invest a certain amount of his energy in flogging a dead horse. In the end, he realizes that his time is better spent elsewhere on more profitable ventures. With the passage of time, debts heal themselves.

Finally, in any transaction, there is the cost of the transaction and the hoped-for profit. The initial cost is real, but the hoped-for profit is a thought-form. As a debtor, this gives you additional leverage. Business people hate to lose their initial outlay because those dollars are then lost forever and cannot be used to generate additional business in the future. But often they are prepared to lose, or to not make, the profit they had hoped for. This enables you to do deals to settle your debts by paying only a percentage of what you owe. Further, you have the possibility of not paying with money. You can barter. You can offer to do work for nothing and pay it off that way. You can take a debt that's owed to you and pay off a bill by getting the creditors to accept that in payment. Lots of options are open to you.

In passing, let's talk for a moment about interfamily debt, money that has been lent to or borrowed from your loved ones. The family is a powerful metaphysical unit into which we incarnate in order to learn about life. Its value is that it creates a protection around us and allows individuals to work out their karmic stuff in a friendly setting. I believe in reincarnation. In any family setting there will be, metaphysically, eons of accumulated karma and situations that can all get sorted out in the space of just a few years. The beauty of the family unit is that it is a hotbed in which we learn about love. And love, in the end, is the saving grace of humanity.

In that light, how can we let family debt come between us? I believe that you don't owe your family anything, and they in turn don't owe you. Whatever financial transactions have been incurred are part of the great karmic melting pot into which you and your family members have been cast. If you accept the theory of reincarnation, there is no way of knowing who owes what to whom. It's sad, therefore, if you can't visit your Mum 'cos you owe her a grand or two. The family creditor is as trapped as the family debtor because the emotion of interfamily debt often creates such difficulty. For you all to become free, you will have to sort it out. The best solution is for everyone in the family to forgive everyone else. So you go to your close relative and tell them straight, "I love you, but you ain't getting it. You will have to forgive my debt. This family needs to be free."

In a world where the common people are so manipulated and controlled by the system, the family should stand as a symbol of spirituality and self-reliance—it should be loving, strong, and free. It's important that the combined strength of that unit should be used by its members to liberate themselves, not to bind each other. If everyone were magnanimous and understood things from a more infinite, loving perspective, true heights of spirituality and joy could be attained. Either way, whether they will forgive your debts or not, I'd walk away and forgive myself.

Of course, not all interfamily transactions create negativity. If an arrangement is loving and helpful, and everybody's happy with it, then see it through. But so often this is not the case. Part of your intention should be to face that fact and fix it!

The thing is to heal yourself before the pressure of all your financial commitments makes you ill and therefore useless to yourself and others. We are only here in this life for a short time—23,000 days, maybe. Why would you want to spend any amount of those precious days in a state of anguish over something that is not really real? Money is a thought-form, and so is debt. Why mess around arguing, trying to change people's opinions. The bank says you owe; that's its opinion. You have another thought-form that says, "I owe, but you ain't getting it." In the infinity of things, these piddly little arguments are irrelevant.

Of course, if everyone didn't pay, the world would grind to a halt. But the fact is that only a small percentage default. If you have to be among that percentage, so what? By lying on the hospital bed of finances for a while, you can heal yourself and get on with the rest of your life. The force of your *will* is immediately strengthened as you go into a new balance. Then, if that balance is sustained through a financial discipline, it will bring you wealth. Very likely, that wealth will generate work, energy, and enthusiasm for yourself and those around you. So what you took out of the pool (on an energy level) by defaulting on your debts, you can repay later by becoming successful.

Over the next ten years, you will see a massive restructuring of the world's economies. Since the Second World War, the

Western democracies have printed paper money like crazy. Enormous debts have been racked up by the various governments that will never be repaid. One day everyone will have to stop telling themselves a pack o' lies, and the whole thing will have to be sorted out. When that day comes, confidence will temporarily be lost, and we'll go into a dramatic cash crunch. We will experience what the economists call stagflation, which is inflation with zero growth or a negative annual growth. In that situation, anyone with cash in hand instantly becomes king. While prices will be going up in some areas such as food, in others they will plummet. In the 1930s, commercial real estate fell up to 90 percent in some areas. Why spend five million dollars on a beachfront mansion today, when in five or seven years' time you can have the same property for fifty or a hundred grand down?

The point is, if you begin to work your way out of debt and you go to cash, it's never a mistake—cash gives you options. If all your assets are locked in, or if you have no available cash, it restricts you. When the cash crunch comes, fantastic opportunities will be available to you so you need have no fear. Many of the great fortunes of America were created in the 1930s. Entire industries were brought up for just pennies on the dollar.

Of course, everything goes back to what your intention is. If you heal yourself financially and go to cash and have patience, in a few years' time everything that you have ever dreamed of will be yours. But you have to have vision, and you have to be able to read the writing on the wall. In the early 1930s, there were wealthy families in Germany and Austria that read the developing situation as the Nazis came to power. They sold everything at full price and got out of there. In a changing situation, it is not compulsory to get yourself chewed out. There is always plenty of warning. The metaphysically sophisticated will always be LG (Long Gone), as we call it.

The only thing that stands in your way is the clarity of your intention and the clarity of the eagle eye that you bring to your action plan. Let us look at that now.

DOLLAR-DANCE CONCEPT 13

"Becoming rich is a hands-on process."

✦ ✦ ✦

10

The Warrior's Eagle Eye

Clarity of intent allows you to direct all of your energy in the correct direction so that your full power is brought to bear upon the focus of your *will*. It seems to me that most people are easily strong enough to materialize the things they want. It is the lack of clarity in their lives that messes them up.

Our lives are cluttered. Thus, our consciousness, which is the powerhouse of our destiny, has to give a little energy here and there. Nothing comes together quickly or easily.

I have had the honor of being able to communicate to a tremendous number of people, literally millions, and the single thing that I hope I have imparted is the need for ferocity of intent and limpid clarity. What made the Mongols so damn good was that they were very clear about where they were going, and they were fiercely committed. The Mongolian troops went to war with all of their possessions, their wives, and their children. So every battle was fought as if it were the final battle. There was no room for error, for one can't easily retreat hauling one's goats, the wife, and the kids. The warriors set up conditions under which they couldn't afford to lose. So they never lost.

I noticed this in reading and studying their history. I was fascinated by the honor by which the warrior lived, for he stood just within his own individualism. He needed no prop. He became totally self-sufficient by the sheer strength of what he was. I thought that if we could teach people the same eagle-eyed clarity and force of *will*, and if we laced that with a modern magic (given that we understand the mind so much better than did people of the 12th century), we could build a silent empire of individuals who would conquer the earth on an energy level. That is, not to bind or pillage it, but to use their power to finally set themselves and others free.

So I developed my five-day intensive, "The Warrior's Wisdom," and designed it so that the participant's ego or personality has no real way of resisting. I realized that to build someone into a very smooth, clear personality, you have to strip down the old framework. Rather than replace it with dogma and mumbojumbo, you replace it with nothing, leaving the person almost bare, standing inside a free zone of uncluttered energy. If you then force them to see that their fear is mostly illusion, that they can use that fear as an ally, then they become swift and strong. Once they are clear about their intention in life, that is all they need. They become like Ninja assassins, for whom nothing but the target exists.

Luckily I was right in my guess, and the techniques proved themselves over and over. "The Warrior's Wisdom" became one of the most unusual and powerful seminars anywhere in the world. You don't necessarily need the "Warriors"; all you need is the desire to become more than you currently are.

Here's an analogy I like. Imagine yourself swimming at the bottom of a pool when something very powerful grabs your leg and holds you under water. You have a minute or two to force yourself free of its grip or you will drown. What would be the level of your desire to reach the surface? How much effort would you expend to break free of its clutch, to breathe fresh air once more? Imagine it. Then see if your desire to break out of your current circumstances is as strong as that or less strong. For it often seems to me that stripping down and breaking away takes a massive amount of personal power and courage.

As you detach emotionally from life, you will naturally drift away from those you know and love. You will find yourself out on your own. That can be scary. People would rather live in a jail with their mates and the things they know than to be free, but on their own.

Unless you strip away most of the emotion in your life, it's hard for you to become really clear about who you are and what your true calling is. You can see how confused people generally are, which confirms—to me, anyway—that clarity is not a concept that many understand.

You are an individual, and you came here on your own as a child, and you will die on your own. The fact that you may live in a community or with your family does not change the solitude of your spiritual journey. By cluttering your life with many things, you soon lose sight of who you are and what you came for.

What gives the eagle its power is its superb sight, not its talons. Your enthusiasm and energy are your claws, but without a "higher vision" you are powerless—you are thrashing around in the forest searching desperately for your bifocals. Vision is the ability to rise above a situation and "read" it accurately.

In any commercial transaction, there are the things that people do and say, and then there is the *energy* of the deal. The *energy* stems from the deep-rooted feelings and thoughts of those involved. The *energy* is also created by the underlying motives in people's actions. Often, what people say is very different from what they are thinking or even what they want. By being clear with yourself and rising above a situation, you can quickly get to the heart of the matter. Alternately, you can see the way things are really going, and you adjust your troops to be in the valley for the time when the other characters finally arrive.

Let's say you're in a complex deal, and you're not sure how the individuals involved feel about it; nor can you see how it will pan out. Try this little trick: Lie on the floor with your head toward the north, and relax yourself into a meditative state—a theta brain-wave metronome tape would help you here. Once relaxed, breathe in and out deeply several times. Imagine as you breathe in that your whole being is puffing up like an air balloon. See that balloon getting bigger and bigger.

Gradually, see yourself lifting off the ground and out of your body so that you are now drifting upwards until you reach a height of 100 miles or so above the earth. At that point, put into your mind the personality or the *feeling* of the central character in the deal that you are reviewing. Then, from that elevated position, swoop down to hover just above events. Look carefully at what is *actually* going on. Be especially concerned to read the way it feels.

Next, place yourself inside the main character, and have him or her talk to you about their real attitude, as it may relate to events. Ask that person any questions that are relevant. Keep it simple. Then enter all the other characters and question them. Keep your mind and opinions out of it, and listen carefully to what they tell you. Remember their answers. Upon returning to the waking state, review what information you gleaned from the exercise. Be careful that you don't negate what you learned just because it is the opposite of what you want to hear.

Each individual has his intellectual self, which is the official P.R. handout that he or she wants everyone to believe. But we also have our *inner self*, which lies deep within us and contains our true motivations and all of those archetypal motifs that form the ground-base of our being. By entering into a meditative state and penetrating another person's feelings and personality, you touch their *inner soul*. It cannot tell a lie or try to fake you out.

To perform this exercise effectively, you will have to have worked upon yourself somewhat so that the clarity of your perception is not muddled by too much of your own stuff. As you view a person in the *inner state*, you should imagine yourself inside them facing out at the questioner. As the person answers, be aware of any shift in feelings. At what exact words did the shift occur? Was the shift positive, negative, or a variation in between? Whereas in the waking state a person's body gives off telltale signs of how that person feels, in the *inner state,* a person's feelings provide the same information, but even more accurately.

In doing this exercise over time, one gets to the point where eventually one doesn't even have to go through the performance of lying down and meditating. This is especially true when the person you are reviewing is there in front of you. As they talk, relax yourself; imagine a pastoral scene with which you are familiar—I see myself floating in or sitting on a mountain lake that I know well.

Then, see yourself standing inside the person's body and reverse that mental image so that it is now looking out at you. Of course if the person you are talking to is there with you, they will most likely be facing you, but if they are positioned at a slight angle, just adjust your mental image to fit the direction in which they are facing. Then, holding a pure concentration uncluttered by input from your own mind, stare with your left eye at their right eye, and while holding the mental image of standing inside them, ask your questions. If at that time they are talking about the deal in question, so much the better, but even if their conscious mind is elsewhere, it won't stop you.

You begin your question with words that will trip the memory recall of their *inner* mind. Let's say the deal under discussion is to build a bridge over a lagoon 12 miles outside Lagos, Nigeria. You would begin your question with three call words, "Bridge, Lagos, Lagoon." That accesses the part of their mind that holds all their feelings about the project. Pause for a split second, then ask your question. The answer comes back to you as their words in your mind.

If, however, the central character in the deal is at another location, go back to the balloon technique. The best time for your review is when he or she is asleep. If, say, the character goes to bed at 10:00 and wakes at 6:00, your best time for this exercise is 4 A.M. in his or her time zone. This is because at that particular time of night, his or her brain activity is at its least active. They are closest to their true self, for the main REM dream cycle that occurs just prior to waking will not have started yet. If you are in a hurry, use the balloon method at any time. Just be sure that as you concentrate upon your target, you have a limpid, clear mind so that you can hold the mental connection long enough to ask and receive the answers you require.

Using this method, you will find that you can pick up people's thoughts. Let me clarify. What I mean is, you will be able to pick up exactly how those thoughts feel to that individual. You may not be able to discern his or her precise thought-form, but you can find out what effect those thoughts are having on the individual in question.

Using these types of techniques (and there are others in my book *The Quickening*) allows you to become a crafty warrior. Many will think *crafty* means "dishonest." I don't agree. Crafty is using all of the resources of your humanhood to put you in a strong position. It does not necessarily mean that you will cheat people. It just means you have power and clarity that few possess.

What attracted me to the old esoteric traditions of Europe was that in those practices there was a power others didn't have. My motivation was not to control, but rather to set myself free. What is the point of putting effort into your quest if the results of that effort bring you nothing in particular? That's why I don't have much enthusiasm for religions. For although they teach some good stuff, they fall short of telling people how to be really powerful. In fact, most religious people tend to be a bit wimpy, for they have given their power away to a musty symbology that exists outside of themselves. The religion becomes more important than they are, and that is the recipe for a long, hard struggle. The occultists that I met, the good ones, all had very powerful, uncluttered concentration. They knew how to hone the mind into a perfect tool of their will. Using their vision, they got what they wanted with little or no effort. Wealth was never an issue, for they read everyone so well that they always won. That is why intent, clarity, and simplicity in your concentration is so vital to you. You can lead a complex life and still have clear simplicity, for you override the complexities with the force of your concentration. To achieve that kind of subtlety in your power, you have to liberate yourself from all the nonsense that has gone before.

Imagine it like this—imagine that someone tied a piece of string to your leg when you were born and that the string was endless. As you traveled about and lived your life, the string wound itself around all the situations you encountered, tangling and knotting itself as you went about. To become free, you'll have to first untie the string from your leg, which means that you have to cast yourself into a void where you exist in a perpetual state of "not knowing," where you exist just with yourself. Then you are obliged to follow the string back carefully, untying it from all the things around which it has become entangled.

At first, this seems to be an impossible task, for perhaps the string has been winding up your life for 30 or 40 years. But as you travel back, you are delighted to find that every so often, by unraveling the string from one snare or obstacle, you unravel it from all the similar situations there have ever been. Large chunks of the string become free and loose instantly.

This is the story of our lives. We spend years tying ourselves into knots, and then one day we either realize that we have had enough and set ourselves free, or we never do realize it. The string becomes a friend, and we die trapped like a fish in a net.

Perhaps I have drifted away from the main theme of this book, which is money making. But when you think of it, intent and clarity are the foundations of your money-making efforts.

Without these, you are almost bound to fail. It's interesting that 60 percent of all small businesses in America go bankrupt in the first ten years.

In looking at that figure, one might see that the owners were inexperienced or undercapitalized, but mainly in the stories of these failures what one sees is that what they lacked was clarity. It is so easy to start a small business without ever looking at what one is committing to or whether or not there is really a strong market for the service or product. After the initial success, one can easily become carried away from the focus of the business. In the day-to-day rah-rah of doing the business, one tends to forget to count the money.

There is no other reason for being in business other than to count the money. I think that every business person ought to have those words in two-foot-high letters draped across his or her office wall. Manufacturing, creating, selling, P.R., and shipping are not the business; collecting and counting the money is the business. That is not necessarily glamorous, but if you are clear, you will know that basically there isn't anything else. If you don't concentrate on counting the money, people soon realize that money is not the focus of your consciousness, so they give you everything other than money: kudos, acclaim, praise, etc., etc. And sooner or later you'll be in trouble.

The other thing that I am sure is true is that many of the owners of these small businesses never really thought through what they were letting themselves in for. I can't count how many people have told me that they want to open a bookstore. Unless you love books and you are prepared to live and breathe them, opening a bookstore is a prison. You have to go down there every day, nine 'til five, and sit there with a bunch of musty books for friends. If it is a small store, you probably won't be able to hire a large staff, and so you will be tied to the place. Imagine a business that stocks 20,000 different items. Just ordering the books is a full-time job. To do that day in and day out, you have to love it.

So before you commit to something, you ought to be very clear about what you are getting into. And to be clear, you have to know what it is that you want.

I have done polls at my seminars, asking the participants: What do you want in life? I was amazed to discover that 70 percent of those questioned did not know what they wanted. I got a lot of vague replies such as, "I want to be happy," "I want to be rich," "I want to find my soulmate," and so on. But very few people in the room ever knew *exactly* what they wanted and how they were going to get it.

In fact, the results of those surveys break down into 70 percent don't know, 20 percent have a fair idea of what they want but no real idea of how to get there, and only 10 percent know what they want and have a good plan for making it happen.

Now think about the Universal Law. It reflects to you exactly and precisely what you put out. If your thought-forms say, "I haven't got a clue about what I want," the Universal Law is going to say, "Listen, mate, if you haven't got a clue, neither have I."

I know that in the old religions it is popular to think that God is up there pulling the strings, deciding who's going to make it and who isn't. But that idea is tribal and childlike. The fact is, the Great Spirit is impartial and allows us to be as silly as we want to be for as long as we want. It does not decide for us. People who have clarity and intention make it in life; those who lack those qualities usually don't make it. It is as simple as that.

First, you should decide what it is that you want. Break it down into short-term goals, mid-term aspirations, and the long-term view. Next, decide to cut out everything from your life that is not a part of the plan. That allows you the power, clarity, and focus to empower just your plan. By getting rid of the attachments and confusions, you make your plan important. To succeed, it is vital that all of your ducks be heading in the same direction.

It follows naturally that every time you direct your focus onto the plan, it gains power. By watching your life carefully, you will soon see if you have clarity or not. For example, let us say that today's goal is to go out and sell five refrigerators. You get into your old clunker rust bucket of a car, and it won't start. So you spend an hour tinkering with the carburetor, and when you finally make it into the marketplace, you're exhausted. Obviously, the car is not a part of your plan. Junk it. Get a little car, with small monthly payments—one that runs. Whatever resources you have, they must be invested in the plan. If you won't invest in yourself, who will?

Next, take a look at the quality of the people who surround you. Do these people back you emotionally, or not? If they don't back you, are they at least passive? If not, get rid of them. Sometimes it is hard to drop off your mates at the great bus stop of life. But remember, your energy will only rise in direct relationship to the number of things you are able to get rid of—not to the things you acquire. By getting rid of things, attitudes, encumbrances, and blocks of one kind or another, things fly.

Next, if your plan calls on others to help you, be very sure that those involved are clear as to what their duties are and what is happening. Don't forget that generally people are as thick as two planks and asleep for the most part. Also, they are not clairvoyant. You need to let them know what you want, and you have to be consistent and clear. You might say, "Stack these crates by the gate," and they will nod and say, "Yes." But that does not mean that they have understood or that they will follow through correctly. Further, you'll find that they will stack the crates correctly Monday through Thursday, and on Friday you'll arrive to find all the crates on the roof.

In dealing with people, never presume that they know what they are doing. Every so often you will be delightfully wrong, and a genius will show up. But for the most part, people range from fairly incompetent to utterly useless. This applies to professional people, as well as to the ordinary working folk. Just because a fellow has a business card that says he's passed his accountancy exam doesn't mean that one should take it for granted that he knows what he's doing. Many don't.

If you are starting a business, people will tell you that what you need is a good lawyer and a good accountant. That is probably the last thing you need. I have yet to meet an accountant who knows half as much about my business as I do. How could he? If you are going to start a business, get your plan together, test the market, check and double-check your ideas, and head out.

Once you are making money, you'll need the accountant. But his function, for the most part, will be to add up the figures and to fill in the forms that tick-tock requires of you. Think of this— if the accountant were any damn good at developing a business, why would he sit in a back room filling out forms? He wouldn't. The good accountants are out there doing it and getting rich. The rest are adding up the forms. Eventually, when you make a lot of money, you will need a good accountant. Hire the very best, never mind the cost. Every penny you spend will be worthwhile. Making money is a piece of cake. Holding on to it and investing what you have made is a major problem for almost everyone.

The point to remember is that in dealing with people, never presume anything. Clarity of communication is vital. The rule is to repeat everything three times and check it four. In that way, as you entrust parts of your plan to others, you feel secure.

As your plan grows, and more and more people become involved, your main function will be to be a motivator. The average person can concentrate on something for about two minutes. Unless you are on top of the situation hour by hour, day by day, your people will soon drift into "busy work" that consists of piddling about doing nothing in particular. In any business, there are jobs that are productive and sometimes confrontational, for they test you. And then there is all the other work, none of which earns any money. People avoid the confrontational, productive stuff as much as possible, and they head for the "busy work" as if it were a pile of free doughnuts.

It is vital, therefore, that you stay in touch—not only with yourself and your goals—but also with the people around you. You need to let them know what is important to you, and you have to ensure that they concentrate on the productive stuff as much as possible. The problem is that they will constantly run away like little kids. And so a part of your time and effort will be to haul them back by the ear and repeatedly indicate to them what is vital and what is not.

It is not surprising to me that so many talented people go down the pan as they try to expand a one-man operation into a major commercial outfit. When you first start, your creativity is paramount, but eventually your ability to motivate and manage people will be more important. It's pointless to be a great bio-chemist if you can't hire a competent bookkeeper. Unfortunately, our educational system does not really train people in skills that they need in life. It is almost impossible to hire a typist who can type a hundred words a minute. I have hired bookkeepers—several—who I discovered could not operate a common calculator. They didn't last long. It's mind-boggling, really, especially when you think in terms of who it is who's going to look after these people. If we create a society of mental paraplegics, the down-drag of this responsibility will completely undermine the Western democracies. It is easy to see why Japan is scooping the pool.

It seems to me vital that, as you expand to include others, you become good at picking strong people. I don't have all the answers to these problems, but my way is to surround myself with just a few people and to subcontract everything. That way one can run a number of large companies, each with half a dozen people. I choose Mongols, as I call them. I don't so much care what a person knows. What I look for are people who are unstop-pable. I like people who can ride through a certain amount of pain and discomfort to reach their target. They have to be dedicated to themselves first, then to the common cause—which in our case is publishing. If they can't walk through fire, literally, I don't want them. So we light up a bonfire to 1,200 degrees Fahrenheit, and we get the whole company to walk across barefoot, young and old alike. We do this several times a year. When a person can walk through searing hot coals and not flinch, then shipping 60 boxes by 11 o'clock is no more than flicking a fly off a cake. You need warriors—strong, limpid ones—and you can conquer the earth. It takes focus.

💰 DOLLAR-DANCE CONCEPT 14 💰

"There is no other reason for being in business than to count the money. Manufacturing, creating, selling, P.R., and shipping are not the business— collecting and counting the money is the business."

When I started my publishing company in the United States, I simultaneously opened one in Australia and England, as well as a small venture in Canada. I would call my foreign associates, and they would spend 20 minutes on the phone telling me that they had painted the roof green. At the beginning, I was polite. I listened to that stuff. But later I wanted to get everyone focused, so I would begin every conversation with the question, "How many, how much?" If you are a publisher, that is all you really need to know. For there is nothing to the business other than how many products did we produce, and what did we sell them for?

It took my associates a bit of time to get it, bless 'em. But in the end, everyone came to understand the game. The more we focused on "how many, how much," the more success we enjoyed. After a fairly slow start, in which it seemed we trotted across the parking lot of life with one shoe on and the other shoe off, we finally got clear. We developed one of the only really international New Age trading companies in the world. It wasn't very long, maybe three years, before that company also became one of the largest of its kind in the world.

Looking back, I can see that we made no real progress until everyone got clear as to what the target was. When we first started, we all felt that community service—helping people—was the goal. But after a while we realized that there were more people who needed help than we could ever possibly hope to assist. Our limited resources were used to communicate with people. But from those people we didn't really earn a profit, we just earned gratitude. And if you want to help the world, that is probably what will happen to you. You will break even or at best make a small profit, and that is it.

However, when my associates and I looked into our hearts, we could see that what we wanted was to be wealthy, *as well as* to help people. Soon we realized that money—lots of it—would assist us. First, money would help us feel good about ourselves; and second, having more resources, we could do a better job. So we focused on money, and we got what we wanted. Once we were clear, we never looked back.

It is important, therefore, that you constantly evaluate your inner motivations so that your quest is empowered by truth. And as those inner motivations change, it is easy to lose sight of what you are going for. If you get too far off track, it will make you miserable. All the success in the world is useless if you are unhappy.

Let's say that you want to be a millionaire. That may be true. But if you think it through, creating a million dollars will also create a lot of ties and obligations that will bind you. Perhaps what you want is freedom. You may be extremely disappointed to discover that a million is not a lot of money nowadays, and it may not get you what you want. In fact, ten million is the minimum needed to get you the liberty you seek. Then there is the drag that the ten million creates, for it will need looking after.

Perhaps all you need is to prove to yourself that you have worth, that you are a good person, that you *can* contribute. You don't need a million for that. You have only to begin to see value in the things that you do, and bingo, your emotional needs are met. Focusing and granting value to your life and your actions is a prayer unto the sanctity of self. The toil and effort involved in living has to become worthwhile, and unfortunately nothing can make it worthwhile until you grant that realization to yourself.

That is why I teach people to concentrate on themselves, not on others. For you will never relax and become safe until you are strong, very strong. All the money in the world cannot stabilize you spiritually or emotionally, nor can it really dampen your fear. It just allows you to be terrified in a comfortable setting. Nothing else.

It twangs an emotional chord to watch people waffling on about saving the world when the very same people are mired in their own hopelessness. If only they would see that they *are* the God-force, that the greatest prayer they can offer up is their dedication and strength. All the nonsense talked about, God wants this and God wants that, is ludicrous. It's fodder for the feeble-minded. There is honor in your quest. There is a spiritual beauty that stems from the perpetual insecurity of life. Confronted by this, we can but accept that it is so and offer up humility in the face of it. Concentrating on where we find ourselves and on making that honorable and worthwhile allows us to accept that the incredible journey on which we have been cast has meaning. We can but hope that at its end we will look back and finally understand what it meant. Why did we come to this strange lump of rock at the corner of the universe, and what did it mean?

If your life, your body, and your mind are not revered and made special by you, then the whole journey becomes one of protest. It becomes a life of confrontation rather than of a peaceful acquiescence in which you accept your place in the great design of all things and confirm this spiritual realization by the purity and clarity of concentrating solely on it.

In the light of this realization, everything else is irrelevant, is it not?

The Battle Plan

It is wonderful to dream great dreams, having become clear and having worth granted to whatever it is that you do. You are now faced with the task of carrying those dreams from thought into reality.

Imagine yourself a Mongol general. Today's target is to move 120,000 men and attack Moscow. How are you going to do it? You need a battle plan. You know that you have the resources. You have sent scouts out to ascertain which is the best direction for attack. You know from information received that Moscow has 40,000 defenders. You know also that the city has enough food for 23 days. Given your overriding power and the ferocity of your intent, all you need to take Moscow is a cohesive plan. The attack and capture of today's target will flow naturally, providing you think through your approach. Provided also that you don't shoot yourself in the foot and toss 60,000 men over a cliff, the capture of the target is a foregone conclusion. After riding 6,000 miles, 120,000 Mongols took Moscow in the heart of the winter, in less than a week. The date—January, A.D. 1238.

The Target

Now imagine your life in these same terms. Make up a battle plan. Commit that plan to paper. First, what is the target? Head up your battle plan by writing down the one overriding desire that you have for your life. Under that, in smaller letters, write down whatever secondary desires or needs you wish to materialize. In committing your plan to paper, you make it sacred. The written plan functions both as a tool for order and clarity, and also as a prayer. Create a place in your home where the plan will be kept. Make that place a sanctuary. Perhaps you might want to get a special box, a treasure chest in which the plan will be stored. Place in the box with your plan a few items that hold religious or spiritual value to you. A crystal, an eagle's feather, a picture of Mother Teresa, the petrol cap from your guru's Rolls, whatever. The point, symbolically, is that you will never detach your efforts in the physical world from your overall quest and spiritual search. However mundane today's events might be, they still form a thread in the tapestry. It is important never to forget that.

By the bye—and nothing to do with the plan—I think any guru who doesn't have a Rolls Royce is a scumbag. As we plod along on our quest to become strong, we need symbols, symbols that are larger than life. How can you get worked up over some scrawny twit in a loincloth, wobbling about on a bicycle? To make it, you have to set your sights big. The guru should symbolize "making it in life." If you follow some potless idiot, you'll tend to adjust your aspirations downwards so that you don't race ahead of your spiritual leader. Instead of making it, you'll wind up with a puncture repair shop in the back streets of Karachi. Forget it! I want my guru to be fat, rich, and happy.

Back to the battle plan. In order for your plan to be dynamic and alive, you will need to refer to it daily. Doing so regularly becomes a form of meditation in which you use the power of your mind to empower the plan. All major events that form a part of the plan should be noted and written down. Adjustments can be made and successes recorded. Think of it as a chord of music, a tone poem, offered daily to the Gods of Liquidity. That chord should resonate throughout your being so that you are the plan and the plan is you. It becomes the most important thing in your life because you have decided that it is so. By reviewing the plan constantly, you never lose sight of your target.

The Resources

Next, sit down in a quiet place and really take stock of what resources you have. Perhaps you can write them down on your battle plan in different-colored pens so that they stand out and don't slip from your memory. Don't look at your resources only from a financial point of view, for what you are is so much more than the money you may or may not have. Think in terms of the sum total of the energy you have available to you. That life force that runs through your body and your mind is the most powerful and valuable thing that you have. It is a God-given resource that can be translated into excitement, honor, quest, and happiness. Parts of it can be expressed for the good of the world, and other parts can be expressed in the marketplace and sold for cash.

Think in terms of what knowledge you have, and constantly review what use you have made of that knowledge. More than likely, you have talents and ideas that you have never taken advantage of. Perhaps the secret of your success is to stop doing some humdrum nonsense that just pays the rent and to embark instead on developing and marketing the talent that lies within you. If you can get excited about your creativity and your life, you can build enough energy around you so that it pulls you away from today's circumstances and into a whole new life. It may take courage to step out and commit yourself, but in the end, boldness will pay off. Fortune favors the brave.

Looking carefully at the energy around you, you will discover yourself to be infinitely richer than you think. A part of the energy contains your enthusiasm and the life experiences you have gained, but also within it are the connections and friendships you have made. These connections should be cultivated, made special. Sooner or later, you will need a hand up in life, and one of these people, or perhaps a person that you have yet to meet, will be the one to provide you that assistance.

If you don't have friends or connections, I would make the acquiring of some a number-one priority. If going out and meeting people in uncomfortable for you, then I would suggest that you push through that discomfort. Master it as a part of a new discipline. By making the effort to cultivate connections, what you are saying is that you are prepared to expend energy on behalf of your cause. It is an outgoing affirmation that you are looking and searching. When you are doing so constantly, the energy around you changes, and eventually reality responds to your search by granting you unexpected opportunities. Unfortunately, in our world today, real success depends not so much on WHAT you know or even on how good you are. Rather, it depends on WHO you know. That's a fact.

Reviewing your resources from time to time is vital, for it allows you to take stock and to live in the truth. But also it helps you make the resources you do have into something special. It is a point of spiritual strength to give thanks for what you have. There is a tendency for our imaginations to live constantly in the future, concentrating on what we don't have and completely forgetting to acknowledge what has been acquired or achieved. Where you are and what you are right now has to be made right, even if you don't like it that much. Nevertheless, it is you. By criticizing and negating the current circumstances, what you are saying is that you are not okay. What is around you is only an extension of who you are. Look at those things and realize that they are what they are, imperfect though they may be. By accepting the truth, you propel yourself into better circumstances. By resisting, you live in the constant negativity of your own dissatisfaction. Who needs that?

To make every little thing special is to grant a magical quality to your life. Once your life becomes *charmed* in such a way, whatever blocks you may have experienced in the past melt in the light of that inner energy pouring from your heart. From a businessman's point of view, this is beautiful, for everything you touch turns to gold. Further, it helps you to believe in yourself. In seeing worth all around, you make your every act an affirmation of your strength.

Finally, among your resources you may have a certain amount of capital. Money is like manure: You have to spread it about in order for things to grow. If you hold on to your capital for fear of loss, you'll achieve little or nothing in life. There has to be a certain amount of calculated risk. You can't set yourself up for the big win unless you commit a percentage of your cash— or even all of it on occasion—to achieving that win. Think of your dollars as troops. Use them wisely. If you lose a few on the way to Moscow, so what? If you're scared of losing or are uncertain about circumstances in the marketplace, then spend your time evaluating, checking, and double-checking, and you will have your answer. It is the lack of knowledge that creates fear. Once you really know what you are doing and have researched the market or venture you are getting into, then all fear melts in the light of reason.

I know people who live dismal, rotten little lives, yet have hundreds of thousands of dollars on deposit at the bank. I have no respect for those characters. Fear paralyzes them into helplessness. In life, you have to trust people to a certain degree or you live in perpetual negativity. It is better that you get ripped off from time to time rather than imprison yourself in a state of lack. Take risks. Have a go. Just the excitement of being involved is often worth a loss or two. As long as you win most of the time and you're happy, what else could you be looking for?

The Terrain

A Mongol general would never commit his troops without first reconnoitering the terrain. Similarly, you should look over your battle plan to see if you have granted yourself every possible advantage. What are the conditions in which you hope to operate?

Coming from a metaphysical bent as I do, I tend to look at the *energy* of things, rather than concentrate on the logic of investment decisions. I *feel* things out. If there is any discord or lack of harmony, I proceed with extreme caution. Mainly, I use my intuition to decide if the people I am investing in will follow through on their commitments or not. If a deal is noble and good, it will *feel* positive and usually comes together naturally. There may be kinks that you have to iron out, but if there is a feeling of flow, the deal will work. If you meet blocks and difficulties, it may be that the deal will still come off. But then how much emotional energy will you spend on an idea just for the ego trip of saying that you battled through, that you won. To shoot yourself in the foot just to prove that you can make it in life in spite of your limp, is nuts. And throwing yourself out of balance just to prove a point is utterly worthless. It is better that you retreat and set your mind to something more pleasing.

As you look at the ambience of your maneuvers, you should evaluate what the conditions are. Do these actions enhance my freedom, or do they lock me in and bury me? The battle plan needs a territory that is wide and fluid, with as few restrictions as possible. If you place yourself in situations where retreat is impossible, you are trapped.

We have talked about timing earlier. Just to remind you, timing in business is one aspect where most people fail. In launching your moves too early, you burst a lot of the psychic power that your moves contain because you are just hanging around waiting. There is a terrible frustration in trying to force things through when the time is not right. Better that you spend a year at the beach, come back on the right day, and have it all flow effortlessly together.

Personally, I like to start ventures in the spring, for the power of growth is metaphysically with you then. I develop and expand in the summer, and trim and cut away in the fall. In the winter I go drinking with my mates and watch the Ginger Rogers movies over once again.

How does one know when the time is right? First, if the time is not right, the lack of flow will be obvious. Second, in dealing with others, you will be able to read whether or not they are up for the project right now or are ho-humming. If they seem uncertain, put them in the ol' Mongolian pincer movement. Qualify them. Make them commit by just asking them, "Are you ready to do this deal today, or is next Tuesday better for you?" If they are not ready, at least you'll know. How many hundreds of man-hours are wasted each year hanging around while external forces jerk one around? It is so simple to cut that manipulative nonsense out by calling people's bluff.

You can watch amateurs make that mistake over and over again. They get into a deal, and because they feel it's the only game in town, they invest their emotions in it so totally that others feel that weakness and manipulate them like crazy.

You can't materialize your plan if you give away your power. By having little emotion and letting others know that you can *walk* at any time, you become strong. People don't dare mess you around. There is no limit to the amount of people or deals available to you. By qualifying people—and always, always calling their bluff—you control at every step.

"Show us yer tits," we used to call it back home. The psychology was that if your Saturday night date would not oblige you with that small favor, your chances for greater success were remote, to say the least.

Don't confuse emotion with intention. Intention is the force of your *will* projected. It is almost entirely devoid of emotion. It is you clearly demanding that life give you what you want. The problem is that through imagination, you can live out your hopes and dreams prior to their being fulfilled in reality. This is, metaphysically, a leaning forward. Too much of that, and your power is lost through the imbalance of leaning. The emotion created by your imagination burns away the psychic tension in your desire. The power, which should provide your every wish, is lost. Nothing materializes. And, you have to struggle like crazy to force things through.

As was said at the beginning of this book, making money is part of your quest in life. It is a game that you play with yourself. It is only a thought-form, and depending on how strong that thought-form is and on how good you feel about yourself, results flow naturally. It takes a certain aggression, and it takes appropriate action in the marketplace, but that is all. There is no defined limit as to how much money you can acquire in what little time. If any definition exists, it does so just in your mind and in your emotions. When those aspects change, such a flood of abundance takes place that you will be amazed. You wonder where you have been all your life, and you wonder why the hell you came at the project in the past from such a spastic angle.

The trick to money is having some, or at least kidding your mind into believing that what you do have *is* abundance. Once you pull away from all the emotion of money, the block that is created by that emotion is freed. Opportunities flow to you more or less instantly. To make the decision to pull away from the emotion is not hard; after all, the struggle of the past was only an opinion you held. It's no effort to change that opinion. If you "click" your mind so that you see money as energy rather than as a symbol of your survival, you will disengage from baser feelings of the common man and move into a more infinite perspective in which all the wealth that there is in the world becomes yours. What you are and what you have is offered in the same liberated way.

The sacred path—the quest you are on—is then empowered by

all the energy that flows automatically from within. Your infinite view of things overrides the more limited view of ego, and thus you find your life taking on a charmed quality. Everything you touch is magically transformed into a greater feeling of abundance.

In the end, what more will you need than to look back on your life and see a goodness there? To see your goals achieved? To see that there was a higher meaning and purpose to it all.

What will your success and wealth do for you? It will allow you to spend more time with your mates and your loved ones. It will allow you to work upon yourself and become a better person. You will walk away from the prison that most people find themselves in and stand as a free spirit beyond the confines of a world in which little freedom exists. That act of claiming back that freedom of your true self will inspire others to set themselves upon the same task.

When the first human began to read and write, he or she set the world upon a new evolution. Similarly, if a few individuals have the strength and the power to walk away from the restrictions of the world and to stand fearlessly beyond it, eventually, in some distant millennium, all mankind will also come to that same liberation. It will be a special pleasure for you to look back, poised, in some place in eternity, and know that you were there at the beginning of the movement. Your gift was that you realized at an early stage that you were indeed eternal, immortal, and infinite, and that you had the courage to walk with that idea in your heart while the rest of mankind said that such a limitless overview wasn't true or even possible. And what of others? The way they are, is the way they are. And the way the world is, is the way it is. It will change when it is good and ready and not one day sooner. Once you accept that, you can set yourself free to concentrate and empower yourself. Which is why you came here to the earth plane in the first place, is it not?

APPENDIX

Strategies for the Millennium and Beyond

As an afterthought, let us discuss what your strategy might be for the end of the millennium and beyond. Before we do so, let me tell you a couple of things about myself that you ought to know. I am not an economist, nor do I have any financial qualifications. I am neither an accountant nor a stockbroker, and I have no educational qualifications that anyone would recognize, thank God. I do have a great amount of personal history under my belt, though. There is almost no positive human experience that I haven't partaken of. I've been around our planet 97 times to date, and I've figured out how to declare myself in with those forces that are in the thick of things. In commercial terms, I would be considered successful. In my terms, success is energy. I have no way of knowing what level of energy I have attained, and would not want to know, but having developed and worked upon myself over the last 23 years, I've got the "eagle eye" down pat, and life flows more or less effortlessly.

The following pages contain my overview and my preferred

strategy. It may work for you. Or you and your advisors may develop a plan that is more appropriate. The point I am trying to make is that I am not qualified to tell you how to run your financial affairs. I know what I'm talking about, but I feel uncomfortable telling people what they *should* do. Rather, I prefer to suggest ideas for them to evaluate. I might say, "I use this or that technique. It works for me. If you fancy it, try it." After all, everyone's situation is different. How can one offer a catch-all solution with any degree of accuracy?

I believe that as the millennium draws to a close, the world economy will experience a great amount of turmoil. I don't see that as a negative or a positive—things go up, and things go down. The whole basis of the Tao is being in tune with the in-breathing and out-breathing of the Universal Mind.

To formulate a strategy for the millennium, we have to first look at what has happened since the Second World War. After the destruction that took place, governments were eager to get things going again. They developed a liberal money policy to stimulate their economies—America, for example, dished out millions for the Marshall Plan, which aided Europe in rebuilding. In the old days, money was either made from gold or a precious metal, or the paper money was backed by gold. So governments were limited to how much paper money they could print. A pound note or a dollar bill is actually a receipt for the equivalent in gold. On the old pound notes in Britain, it said that the Bank of England would redeem that receipt for gold upon presentation by the bearer. A series of international agreements were concluded earlier this century that freed governments from the gold standard. Further, in the old days, many smaller banks printed their own money. Bit by bit, the Powers That Be decided that printing cash was too valuable a privilege to be left in the hands of ordinary folk. So the right was snatched back, and a monopoly was granted to those forces that were politically and financially powerful enough to establish and sustain that same monopoly.

In the United States, a group of banks joined together to form the Federal Reserve. They then cajoled Congress to grant an exclusive right to their group to print money for the entire American economy. In this way, they hoped to corner the financial markets by printing cash and regulating its flow. This goal was achieved more or less instantly, and this same private club still prints all of the money today, some 80-odd years into the monopoly. Amazingly, there was a discipline about printing and spending that lasted many years. But with the advent of the Second World War, things changed. After the war, people were not prepared to accept conditions that had existed prior to 1939. They wanted and demanded a better life. Politicians responded to these demands by cranking up the printing press. At the same time, the U.S. got involved in the Korean War, which placed an additional strain on its resources while the world was still in the rebuilding stage.

Metaphysically, in all strength there is propensity for weakness and collapse. America had just emerged victorious from the Second World War and played to a fairly decent standoff with the North Koreans. Most of the political, military, and almost all the economic power in the world rested with the U.S. To understand the world economy in the late 1990s, we have to look at what has happened to America since 1945.

Given America's strength after the Second World War, it was not surprising that when the Vietnam situation came up, President Kennedy would naturally think that popping down there to kick a little butt was no big deal. Kennedy was an expansionist at heart. He attacked Cuba and got himself in a mess, and, smarting from that reversal, it was natural that his psyche would create a way to make things well again. One thing about Kennedy was that he had an ego you could haul around on a truck. So the Vietnam excursion was sold to the American people as a jolly good idea. The theory was that a few thousand marines would trot around the bushes growling, and the beastly North

Vietnamese would hightail it back to their neck of the woods. The problem was that nobody had read the history books. The idea was ludicrous. One phone call to Paris would have revealed that 15,000 Frenchmen had tried to do the very same thing at Dien Bien Phu—not many came back. History was ignored, and off the American troops went.

It wasn't long before the American people, "bless their little cottonsocks," got heartily pissed off with Vietnam. It then fell to Tricky Dicky to sort the problem out. Meanwhile, the lads in the bushes were doing their very best, but they also got sorely pissed off with the caper. They felt that they had not been given the tools to finish the job. Taoist philosophy suggests that one should never combat, that you should always retreat in the face of confrontation. But it also suggests that if you have to commit to a battle, you should make damn sure of winning—and quick. One thing about Maggie Thatcher in the 1980s was, like her or not, she didn't mess around. When the little fracas developed with Argentina over the Falkland Islands, she sent the entire British Navy—including two nuclear submarines—to sort things out. Everyone had a marvelous time. The lads got a smashing suntan as they cruised the South Atlantic for a month on the way down there. The queen sent one of her sons, and the whole punch-up was over in a week. Everyone was back in the pub, Saturday lunchtime.

But the Vietnam war was different. It dragged on and on. As it did so, America had to borrow more and more money to sustain its involvement, and by the late '70s, the national debt had been cranked up to about half a trillion dollars. It followed that with all these new dollars swishing about, inflation would hit the roof, and sure enough, in President Carter's time it got totally out of hand.

If you plot the economic history of the U.S., you can see that the mid-1960s were the height of American economic clout. The Vietnam War was the watershed. It was the most important single event of this century. It was a turning point for America, and therefore for the entire world. The billions that the war cost were added to billions that were being spent back home. The government began borrowing money from all and sundry at a rattle-along pace.

Meanwhile, the corporations were not far behind in getting in on the act. All sorts of fancy-sounding instruments were created: junk bonds, debentures, mutual funds, promissory notes of one kind or another, options, futures, shares, and warrants. You name it, and the lads at head office would think it up. Because governments were allowed to turn paper into wealth, it followed that it would be good for the world economy if business folk were allowed to do the very same thing. After all, things had to keep expanding to pay for the interest and mounting debt that America and the rest of the world was racking up. The more people worked and paid taxes, the better governments were able to handle what was now an embarrassing situation.

The importance of the Vietnam War for the American economy cannot be overlooked. Meanwhile, the smaller nations began passing laws that liberally benefited their citizens and gave the working people all sorts of perks without really thinking through how they would be paid for. Paper created the benefits. Politicians were happy, and the people came to expect handouts as a right, not an option. Metaphysically, humans are protected somewhat because our imagination has to be carried physically into reality in order for us to experience events. Thus, negative thinking doesn't immediately manifest itself at our feet. The downside of this protection is that positive experiences have to be built gradually in the same way. But with the advent of paper wealth, corporations, banks, and governments could circumvent our God-given metaphysical protection and instantly turn their imagination and their thought-forms into hard cash. Real worth without any major effort. Herein lies the first chapter of a sorry tale.

When your expansionist mind gets too far ahead of reality, its ability to control and concentrate on events is reduced. There is a point where the tensile strength of a thought-form crosses a critical line. For Hitler, attacking Russia was that line. For the U.S.— and therefore the world's economy—Vietnam was the catalyst. Once that line is crossed, it is only a matter of time before a contraction has to take place. Within the contraction are the seeds of metaphysical safety and survival. The collective inner mind of the planet knows what it needs in order not to self-destruct. Suddenly, for no logical reason, everyone agrees more or less at the same time that it's best to pull back.

I believe that as humans, we all communicate on an inner level all of the time. The Hundredth Monkey concept is offered as proof that such communication exists in the animal kingdom. If this is fact, how much more sophisticated our inner human communication must be. Collectively, we all agree on certain things. On an intellectual level, it is called public opinion. On an inner level, it's like a collective dream from which we all wake on the same morning. Suddenly, for no apparent reason, a new idea enters the world mind. Although that idea may take years to filter into concrete change, once the idea is there and takes root, it becomes a powerful force in the world psyche.

To many, our planet is just a lump of rock hurtling through space. To the metaphysician, it is a living organism that knows what it needs to go through its cycles and reach its final destiny. It is self-evolving and self-regulating. It has a spirit, much in the same way a physical body has a spiritual, metaphysical evolution that exists concurrently with the body's life. When humans mess with the planet's natural balance by, say, polluting the ozone layer, we reap nature's reaction to that infringement. Herein lies chapter two of this tale.

Let's go back to the economic history of America. Plotting a chart from the War of Independence to the mid-1960s, you see that the economy rose and fell at very regular intervals. Expansion and contraction was a part of its balance. Whether you follow Kondrotief's curve or the Elliott wave theory and the Fibinachi numbers, you don't have to be a living genius to see that economy breathes in and breathes out, as does everything else. After all, what is the economy? It is the thought-forms and activities of humans, nothing else. Obviously, it will follow rhythms as we humans do.

In the 1960s, a major shift took place in the U.S.—Flower Power appeared in the collective dream. The birth of new spirituality, a higher consciousness, began to wriggle in its embryonic stage. Back in England, the Beatles took up the world prayer and sang of a higher ideal, a new individualism, a kinder view.

The Flower Power movement in the '60s was simplistic and charming. Look at the humility of its world prayer, "All we are saying, is give peace a chance." *All,* a humble word followed by a plea to the forces of control from the collective mind, offering a new idea, expressing itself in a childlike way. A stunning beauty existed in this major shift, and like so many soft and gentle turns the world makes, the Flower Power movement revolutionized the world. Eventually that transcendence began to change the economic scene.

A tussle has developed between the international forces that are pushing for globalization and more and more government control, and the inner transcendental forces that are pulling people out of the tick-tock system toward more spiritual and financial freedom. The movement to raise one's consciousness coupled with the drug scene and the ecstasy dance movement in Europe has formed an alternative evolution to the old patriarchal military system. Cyberspace and the Internet are additional manifestations of the independent global mind trying to extricate itself from institutional domination. The next 20 years will see an enormous conflict between the old order and the new. Confusion and a lack of purpose or vision will predominate in the global mind.

The lands south of the equator exist as a balance for the planetary organism. They have rested in a kind of sleep state that counterbalanced the frantic activity of the Northern Hemisphere. But in the '60s, those lands to the south began to awaken. Like some massive prehistoric animal frozen in a glacier for a billion years, suddenly the ice melted and the animal rose to its feet. Again, the first we heard from those lands was from their singers and actors. Like the meistersingers of Europe, who heralded the Renaissance, going from tavern to tavern singing of a new chivalry, a fairness brought out from the legend of Camelot, Australia sent its meistersingers out to tell the world that the slumbering giant had risen. South America, meanwhile, also woke up to a new prominence. Because the Flower Power movement had created a massive market for transcendence, and because drugs are but a by-product of that transcendence, South America woke up to its own individuality and development. Having little else to offer, it follows naturally that they would become the farmers and suppliers of the northern drug need.

In getting stoned, an individual does not seek to destroy the status quo. Rather, he seeks to pull away from the evolution of the common man. He is not spiritually aligned to the status quo, and he feels powerless to change things. Therefore, in perhaps a misguided way, he chases after his God-self, hoping to touch upon a new reality—a transcendence—through the use of his drugs. In theory, that shouldn't bother anyone. It s no different from a guy getting drunk. But in practice, it rattles the Powers That Be like crazy. Why? Because the illegal drug industry is as destructive to the status quo as it is to the ordinary individual. Also, it is a massive revenue producer that lies outside the system, thus undermining the forces of control.

Currently, drug revenue in the U.S. amounts to between $400- and $500 million a day—or, over $150 billion a year. That money is not in the hands of the status quo—it's in the hands of fringe-people who were never supposed to have access to wealth. Worse than that, it's all tax free, so its impact in the economy is massive. Drugs have taken the minds of the people away from the "status quo." The cash generated from drugs has liberated an underclass of people, expanding them from often hopeless economic circumstances into a major economic power—so much so that the drug industry is now beyond the control of governments.

When you create circumstances under which millions of people have no chance of economic success and you tax, regulate, and stack every rule to discriminate against the ordinary people, you should not be surprised if they walk away and invent their own system. The drug industry is just one more example of the transformational mind of mankind pushing against the stifling control and attitudes of the ruling elite—attitudes that have been inherited from the Industrial Revolution of the last century.

In the southern lands of Africa, nations awoke and demanded independence. Black South Africans followed that same awakening. In the East, the Indonesians fought a gruesome war with pick-ax and shovel and kicked out the colonialist Dutch. All over the world, the European powers withdrew, as now was the time. The colonialization of the tribal world in the 1700s and 1800s was a metaphysical bridge, a custodianship. It took sleeping tribal nations gradually into a new metaphysics of individuality. But now, the lessons had been learned and the local people graduated, demanding that the teacher leave them to their own destiny. Meanwhile, the transcendence of Flower Power unshackled the world mind. We took a quantum leap in technology.

We dared to dream of new possibilities, and from technology we discovered how to move our minds faster and faster. Computers were developed that could read every page of a 20-volume encyclopedia in seconds. Transcendence expanded the inner mind, while technology expanded the intellectual self.

The female has always been custodian of the yin, inner energy of the world, while the male carried the responsibility of the expansionist yang. But medical technology gave us the birth control pill. The female was freed from much of the restraint that held her in a tight discipline around yin and the family. Through economic necessity and through a natural, spontaneous reaction to her liberation, she headed out from her yin base into the sexual freedom previously reserved under the patriarchal system for men as a yang experience. Once again, the balance in the global mind had shifted. The cohesiveness of the family unit came under pressure.

The Japanese, with their intellectual minds, took to technology like ducks to water. In doing so, they also moved from a yin, Zen, island society, to the yang expansionism of the Western world. Watch how beautifully all these events wrap into a pattern that provides an obvious clue to the future. Notice how it all lies in the perfect symmetry of world evolution. As the lands of the Southern Hemisphere woke up, the balance of the planet changed. There was no longer a yin in the south, to balance the yang of the north. Suddenly we had perpetual yang in the world mind—constant activity, north and south, constant input—no rest, no counterbalance.

Flower Power, the money printing presses, transcendental thought, drugs, Vietnam, computers, the pill, the development of the Asian economies, and the waking of the Southern Hemisphere have disturbed the tranquillity of the inner world mind. There is only so much it can take. Further, the accumulative energy of all this expansionism has undermined the ruling elite so much so that economies are now less easy to control. Collectively, we all agree, on an inner level, that we want peace—both inner peace and peace on an international level. Enough is enough! The ground base of our sanity, our inner mind, has been rattled.

The space shuttle explosion was a manifestation of overexpansion—too much yang and not enough yin for safety. Look at how exquisitely that event mirrors today's circumstances. The parallels are stunning. NASA was pushing to expand its shuttle program. It was forced into constant activity in order to get the money it needed from Congress. With that came an imbalance, manifested as pressure from inside the rocket (the inner mind) pushing against its weakest point, the "O" rings (the physical body). The body succumbed. The flagship of world technology was destroyed. Now look at the crew that perished: a scientist, representing our technological pride (yang); some U.S. military men (yang); a man of Japanese origin (yang); and a liberated female who was also a teacher, a (yang) profession. Brilliant, isn't it? Did people understand what the shuttle disaster was telling them? Some did, some didn't. Did the inner mind of the world get it? Absolutely. It confirmed to us all where things are heading. We all moved closer to a metaphysical consensus.

Then, just to ensure that we got it absolutely, the U.S. stock market exploded on October 17, 1987. It contracted (yin) 500 points in 360 minutes. If I were to guess, I would say we have had one technological explosion, one financial explosion, one sexual explosion (AIDS), and that leaves us looking for a natural explosion to complete the sequence. Perhaps, the destruction of Mt. St. Helens was the first event in the cycle and the others followed, or perhaps that was a random event, and a physical or natural explosion of nature has yet to come. Either way, these signs are as subtle as a "plank on head."

At the time of the contraction at the end of the '80s, the American economy looked rather unwell. There was no way of persuading politicians from mainlining red ink. The presses churned out paper for both Wall Street and Washington while there were still suckers to buy the stuff. But as inflation fell and interest rates came back, the Dow rocketed. America is the most inventive country in the world, and its technological base pulled it out of the trouble that the Vietnam debt created and so things picked up. Through America's technological inventiveness, millions of job were created, the deficit came down, and it restored America's domination of world markets. So in the 1990s, things have looked good economically, and the American stock market headed into the stratosphere, taking the rest of the world with it. Japan has not as yet recovered from its bust, and the Asian markets have been exposed as unsafe, so the U.S. reigns supreme— for the moment, anyway.

The technological boom is very interesting; it is in part the manifestation of the intellect trying for immortality, trying to hold on to its domination of the world's destiny. It's the world-ego saying, If we come up with more and more clever ideas, we will eventually live forever, and we will have an effortless utopia in which the mind and the ego can reign supreme.

The problem with this theory in metaphysical terms is that the more the mind dominates, the more the ego comes into play, and the further people depart from their true inner self. So all the technological advances in the world mean nothing if people feel a spiritual void inside of them. They start to act weird. Life becomes more chaotic, and people's morality goes out the window. Bizarre sexual practices become normal. Dog-eat-dog is the dictate. We become less human and spiritual, and more and more robotic, controlled by the system. Eventually, economic stability is rattled because the vapid world we create by the domination of the mind causes us fear. When we are scared, we lash out. We self-destruct.

What will happen through the millennium and beyond? The inner mind, the collective spirit of mankind, desires to return to the yin, desires to discover itself and raise its energy. The outer, intellectual mind and the elite forces that control the world insist on continuing to expand. Thus, a void develops. Inner reality that underpins the intellect is placed further and further away from events. Eventually, the gap grows larger and larger, and the natural safety and spiritual support of the intellect is lost, for it now rests on a void, leaning further and further away from inner truth. At that point, collapse is inevitable.

When will that be? That question is impossible to answer accurately, for it is a question of psychology and spirituality in the global mind and hard to pinpoint. All that matters is that the recession is bound to take place. On which side of the coin would you put your money? Is the natural spiritual desire to contract going to win out? Or can the unnatural, constant activity of the expansionist side hold out forever? I know where my money is.

Let me say one thing before we talk about the plan. Times of economic contraction are not negative. The fact that someone decided to call the phenomenon a "depression" was their point of view. There should be nothing depressing about it at all. You are on your quest. That is exciting. If you're balanced, your boat floats on a low tide in the same way as it does on a high tide. Better, I'd say, because times of contraction are less tiring than times of expansion.

The plan, therefore, is a strategy concerning a level of awareness, and generally recommends somewhat specific ideas. It's impossible to say to someone, "Buy gold, sell stocks," as the markets swing about so dramatically day to day. Then again, if one has no idea where one is financially, emotionally, or spiritually, how can you advise them? Our needs are different, as are our personalities. The financial resources we have to work with differ, also.

The pivotal point of the plan is to voluntarily contract back to a more inner yin energy, before the system forces that contraction upon you whether you like it or not. How you pull back will depend on your resources and needs. The thing to see is that once you have your needs met and you have enough money to purchase the immediate experiences you want, there is a point where perhaps no more effort is needed. Becoming wealthy is great, but it should be tempered with balance, and it should not be accomplished at the expense of self or the quality of life. It doesn't work to have loads of money if your inner spiritual life is a desert, if you have no freedom beyond chasing more and more cash. Quality of life is as vital as heaps of money.

Further, we have to remember that we come to this world to

learn to love in a dimension that is intrinsically fearful. That's the number-one lesson. You don't want to get rich at the expense of being kind and loving to yourself and others. That's hopeless, and it will get you nowhere in the end. Remember, money can never buy you security—there are loads of rich people who are frightened and insecure. What gives you security is tending to your own needs, including yourself, healing yourself and honoring your life's journey—both inner and outer, by not degrading it or trashing it. In self-love and respect and by turning to face the God-force within you, you reach the security and serenity that money cannot buy.

As the world careens through a yang expansion it cannot sustain, you will see sorrow and sadness grip the global mind like never before—people's psyches will be rattled, and it will become more difficult to sustain your own balance if you are out of control, overextended, or if you have lost yourself in the sea of sludge that makes for the global marketplace. Markets will whip around, so opportunities will abound—you could become very rich very quickly. But in that accumulation, develop a strategy that includes you and your nearest and dearest and the real things of life, and don't eat people as you go along, for love is the only eternal spiritual currency. If you don't love and you are not loved, you are bankrupt.

There is an ongoing argument about what may happen to the economies of the world during and after the millennium. It all hinges on America. One theory says that technology will grow and grow, and the wealth of the world will grow with it. The other says that eventually American debt (which now stands at over three trillion dollars) and the debt of the rest of the world is now so enormous and out of control that no amount of growth will save the day. My bet is that you can't have a perpetually debt-driven expansion—not just because it is an economic impossibility, but because even if it were possible, eventually the planet itself, the organism, will rebel against the pollution and mistreatment that globalization and international trade places upon it. Climate changes might really affect crop production, and supplies of food and natural disasters might occur to balance the effect of the perpetual yang feeling that is being forced into the global mind by governments and big business. It is my view that the soul of the organism that is our planet is connected to the collective unconscious (the global mind) of humanity, and it is not separate from it. I believe that the planet knows what is going on in our minds, and that it is a part of our mind as we, in turn, are a part of its body.

The only thing you can say for certain is that the expansion cannot last forever, so any strategy must include a defensive play, for what happens if everything tries to go belly-up all of a sudden? The other side of the coin is that you don't want to be left out if everything continues to expand for the next ten years or so. You don't want to be like those people who are living in bomb shelters in Oregon waiting for a cataclysm while missing all the fun and games.

If there is a stock market correction, or a full-blown depression, prices fall. Yet, governments might counteract that by printing more and more money to fuel a flagging economy, so in a correction we might enter a period of stagnation and/or an inflationary depression, or just serious deflation. It's impossible for anyone to work it out no matter how many charts they've got—it's all guesswork.

However, in a nutshell, America is the key to everything, and it is over three trillion in debt, with its total liabilities calculated at over twelve trillion. It can't pay that back. Most countries can't pay off their debts. One day, world debt is going to come to a big crunch. I don't buy the theory that technology will dig us all out of trouble, as there is a limit to how much information people need and how much technology they can pay for. Then there is the conflict between the transformational yin forces of consciousness-raising and the yang force of globalization and the patriarchal power base. The institutions, over the years, will lose more and more control, and their ability to manipulate people's lives will change. The push and pull between the two major forces—yin versus yang, softness and quality of life versus hardness and control, is the main story for the next 20 years, coupled with whatever protests the planet as an organism decides to make.

Here is my thinking on things:

Cash Is King

Cash in hand is yin; debt is yang. If you begin to sell off assets, settle your debts, and go to a cash basis, you have options. If you are stretched to the limit in the current expansionist mode with little available cash, you are mirroring the rest of the world. Any downturn in the economy, and people will be scrambling to get out. It will be like a thousand people all heading simultaneously for the revolving door of a hotel.

By developing savings and turning assets into cash, you have freedom. Whatever happens, there will be places in the world where the economy is thriving and where opportunities abound. With money in hand, you will be able to buy up assets for pennies on the dollar. The banks will be like supermarkets. They will have repossessed so much stuff that you'll be able to pop over and get a plane, a train, and an apartment building in ten seconds flat. After the crash of '87, you could pick up a building at pennies on the dollar. When things are tough, having ready cash is vital and profitable.

The other reason for having cash in hand is that if you are unemployed, you will need some fall-back money. How much depends on your budget. I recommend at least six months of your current wages. Some people have asked, "If there is going to be a period of inflation, why would you want to be liquid?" Since the value of money will be going down, first, as was said, you don't know if a correction is going to be inflationary or deflationary. In the meantime, you have to eat. Also, with cash in hand, you empower your consciousness and you feel more confident. That is not necessarily the case if you have loads of debt, some assets, and no cash. In the end, cash or a credit balance in a reputable bank is all that counts. If you've got cash, you can make selective investments that will go up rather than being stuck in today's investments that may possibly go down. And, finally, there is nothing stopping you turning some of your cash back into assets at any time the situation looks juicy.

What do you do with your liquid assets? I would put some in a safe deposit box. I would suggest you put the rest on short-term deposit at a reputable international bank, or you could purchase government bonds or T-bills. However, that might expose you to problems if the government tries to restructure its debt. At least some of your cash should be under the mattress. You never know when you will need instant cash for some juicy little opportunity that won't wait till the bank opens the next day. Also, I have always been keen on the ability to get to the airport in a hurry. Remember, freedom is made up of the number of choices you have and the level of your mobility.

Real Estate

In times of contraction, real estate prices tumble precipitously. This is because the business of real estate is not really one of bricks and mortar. Rather, it is an industry related to finance. Very few people buy houses for cash. They need loans to complete their purchases. When there is a crisis of confidence, money is hard to borrow at any interest rate. As people fail to make mortgage payments, the real estate market is glutted by foreclosures. Therefore, prices for an average home in a contraction could easily fall 50 percent or more.

Does that mean that you should sell your house right now? It depends very much on whether you have any assets other than your house. If you don't, then definitely sell, or else immediately get a chunk of equity out of the house in the form of a home equity loan. But if you live in a great neighborhood and don't want to move, then keep the house. You are going to have to live somewhere, and perhaps the value of the house is irrelevant if you wouldn't sell it anyway.

In a contraction, commercial real estate is dead duck. Prices can fall by up to 90 percent. Do you sell, or do you keep it? First, what is the level of debt in the building? If your debt is low, you may want to keep it and ride out any possible contraction. If the building is in good condition and you have an excellent tenant and an unbreakable long lease, the building may provide a steady income for years to come. But if the above conditions are not so, then get the hell out of there fast. You never want all your money stuck in one place.

In a contraction, you will see people returning to their families. More people will be living in the same house, pooling their resources. Apartment rents will fall as people vacate and go to cheaper or shared accommodations. But again, people have to live somewhere. If you have an apartment building in good condition and can run it successfully, even at lower rents, you may wish to keep it. Of course, if you sell today, you may be able to buy it back again in three to five years for much less. My feeling is, watch the market carefully and don't be afraid to sell if things begin to look a bit dodgy. You can always buy things back. Remember, even if you find that you have to sell at a discount to the market price, cash gives you options.

When interest rates are low, pent-up demand will push real estate up, and, of course, high inflation shoves the prices up, also. But real estate is a type of "pass-the-parcel" game for grownups. When the music stops, those holding the parcel are stuffed. So it's risky. However, there are more real estate millionaires in the world than in any other industry. So if you are in real estate, you have to be fleet-footed, and you have to be able to sell when the time is right. I have always lived by the adage that it is never wrong to make a profit.

Land

Land has been a great investment in Europe during the '90s as the European Union has been throwing money to farmers like confetti. How long that will go on is uncertain. The problem with land is that it costs you money to own, and often it does not pay you an income. What gives land a rising value is that people want it to build on and develop. But, with the modern rules and regulations for building becoming harder and harder to get around, you'd better be sure the land you've got isn't going to run into trouble with planning and so forth. This is a very great problem in Europe and Australia, although building permits are much easier to get in America.

Farming land is another area I would personally avoid, because I don't know anything about farming, and I would hate to dole out many hundreds of thousands of dollars only to find that the greenhouse effect turned my investment into a desert. Also, there is worldwide movement to restructure farm subsidies, so crops may not be worth what you think they are once the subsidies are cut. However, everyone has to eat, so I'm sure that some farmers will thrive and do very well, especially if they have healthy crops in times of rising prices. But I would not go into that crapshoot unless I really understood the game.

There is a strong case to be made for the idea of owning a little homestead with, say, 20 fertile acres and a good water supply. The theory is, that in a depression, urban folk will run amok, and there will be rioting in the streets. A little spot on the edge of the woods out of the fray will give you the possibility of growing food and staying safe. I don't disagree with that, but I am not a

survivalist at heart. I feel that the negativity of that kind of thinking only pulls aggravation to you. If you bury a year's supply of
dry food in the ground, you are saying, metaphysically, that your
energy is going to find itself in just such a breakdown. It becomes
an affirmation of lack and helplessness. That intensifies the
thought-form, and something comes along to prove you right. A
moose trots over to your stash and pisses on it! In metaphysical
circles, it's called Moose-Piss Syndrome.

The greatest defense is hard cash. Someone somewhere will
have plenty of food, and even though the prices may have gone up,
if you have cash you can just outbid everyone else and buy it. I just
don't see a depression or correction being so bad that you'll have
to retreat to the hills. Now, if you like the countryside and you like
tinkering in the vegetable patch, then by all means go for the homestead idea. Personally, in a crisis I'd be downtown. There's money
to be made contracting with the city to clean up the mess.

A final point on the theory of riots and social disorder: I'm
sure that kind of thing will happen, but not a lot more than it does
now. In the last depression, America had an average unemployment rate of 25 percent, which means 75 percent were at work
and were able to keep things together. In the little New Mexico
town I lived in, we had 25 percent unemployment the entire time
I was there. There was no rioting in the streets. People are
resourceful, much more so than the bureaucracy would give them
credit for. They figure out how to get by and enjoy it. Because of
the town's beauty and magical atmosphere, people move there
from all over the U.S., particularly to experience being self-
unemployed. They don't want to work too much, and why should
they if they can make it without doing so?

Currencies

If your lifestyle is not international, I would not worry too much about the levels at which various currencies fluctuate. All you will ever need is plenty of your own local stuff. However, for the import-export trade and for those of you who have international investments, currency values are of extreme importance. One general caution I want to offer is this: Anytime there is a downturn in the economy, the first thing governments do is to restrict the flow of money out of the country. Exchange control laws are passed, forcing local citizens to hold on to a falling local currency. You can't imagine how devastating that can be unless you've personally been through it. A Mexican family that had, say, the peso equivalent of $100,000 U.S. in savings, before the crash of their currency, saw that amount eroded to just $330 after the peso had finished falling. Currency control is a fairly predictable phenomenon. In fact, the majority of countries in the world have some kind of exchange control right now, even though things are booming.

I would take a hefty bet that the U.S. and many of the major trading nations will adopt exchange controls sometime in the next ten years. My suggestion is that you shift a part of your assets into other currencies, which, again, gives you options. It's dead easy to open a Swiss bank account, and what most don't realize is that you don't have to go to Switzerland or even to a Swiss bank. You can have an account in Swiss francs in almost any bank in the world. You nominate what currency you want your cash held in when you open the account. The bank should be outside your own country so that your money is not trapped by your local exchange-control laws. Holding Swiss francs in New York would do an American citizen no good, for if he or she wanted to change those francs back into dollars in order to spend them, those dollars would be inside the U.S. and subject to the exchange control laws. It's interesting that by law American banks are not allowed to tell their customers that they offer foreign currency accounts. Such accounts are not illegal, it's just that American banks are not allowed to promote foreign currency accounts to their American clients. Now that tells you something, does it not?

An external account at a bank is one that is held by a nonresident of that country, so a Frenchman holding D marks in a Dutch bank would not be regulated by any restrictions that France might impose on its people. Of course, once the euro becomes the only European currency, then residents of Europe will have to hold their external money in a currency other than the euro. The tactic is to establish an external account someplace while it is still legal. You just call the local branch of a foreign bank in one of your major cities and ask them to refer you to one of their branches back in their home country.

What currency do you want to be in? That is more simply answered by eliminating those currencies that you definitely don't want to hold too much of. The U.S. dollar is very strong at the moment, but it's bound to come under pressure eventually, and it may fall substantially. A dollar-denominated currency such as the Canadian dollar is linked so much to the U.S. that it doesn't really have a destiny of its own. So if you are going into dollars, you might as well be in U.S. dollars rather than Canadian dollars. Although Australia is prosperous and the Australian dollar has been okay for some time, the country is very poorly managed by its government. To give you an idea, Brazil, with 110 million people, has a $100 billion debt; and Australia, with its 16 million people, has almost a $200 billion debt. The Aussie dollar will do well around the year 2000, as Australia is hosting the Olympics, but long term, the Aussie dollar is very linked into world commodity prices.

One thing about Australia that has always attracted me is that it is very safe and a long way off. If there were ever any serious trouble in Europe or America, Australia is a nice, sunny place for your money. In the meantime, New Zealand (NZ) is a safe and peaceful place in which to invest. But I would not put too much in the NZ dollar, as it doesn't have the commodity-based appeal of the Aussie dollar.

The Swiss franc is very safe and strong, and there are no current plans for Switzerland to join the euro, so I imagine the Swiss franc would survive almost anything. The disadvantage is that accounts in that currency pay little or no interest. However, if world currencies come under pressure after the millennium and the Swiss franc holds steady, you have your profit right there. The tactic of an external account is not motivated so much by a desire for income—it is a way to ensure that you are not trapped inside your own currency.

At the time of this writing (late 1997), the Japanese have not recovered from the blowout of their economy and the collapse of assets prices. It very hard to say long term where the Japan yen might settle. The whole point is that currencies are becoming more and more worthless as governments mismanage things to suit themselves, so it's a crapshoot. You could make millions betting right. But my view is to have a little money elsewhere. It's a safety thing.

In the '60s and early '70s, the pound sterling fell out of favor because of problems with various Labor governments. However, in recent years, the British pound has come back like gangbusters. The problem is that right now the pound is wanted as a defense against the euro, and Britain's labor government has promised not to join the euro just yet. But eventually, Britain will be in the euro, and the agreements have already been signed, so you'll be able to swap a fairly solid well-managed pound note for a highly dubious euro.

The object of all these agreements is to disempower nation-states and make everyone subject to an anonymous bureaucratic empire that regulates everything and controls everyone while milking ordinary people to sustain the control mechanism. The same policy operates throughout the democratic world. One day we'll have to have a system that includes the rights of the people to make money and keep it, rather than a system where you can vote for the fox or the wolf, but there's no little box that endorses the chickens. Our time will come, you can be sure of that.

Stocks and Bonds

Recently, the stock markets have been at their highest ever. Interest rates are low, and so is inflation, and that's been good for stocks. However, an entire industry exists to hype stocks up, so the value of companies on the various stock exchanges is bloated out of all proportion. Price earning ratios are up over 15, meaning the stock is trading at 15 times earnings. But if you calculate what the stock costs in relation to the after-tax dividend you might receive, you'll see that many stocks are trading at 40 or more times the net dividend you get. So it would take you 40 years to get your money back. The theory is that companies become more valuable over time and that there's another guy up the road who will pay an even higher price for little or no income and loads and loads of risk. If a company pays, say, just over 3 percent dividend, which is normal in today's market, you'd get about 2 percent after income tax—that's not much. Now factor in a few percent inflation, and your after-tax, after-inflation income is more or less zero. I have never understood how the system keeps going, and it's odd that no one has noticed that shareholders aren't getting anything worth having, while company principals and directors are making a fortune at the shareholders' expense. One day the bubble must burst—it has to.

I think a reasonable dividend would be about 10 percent, with price earnings ratios at around 6 or 8. That would more than halve the world stock markets overnight. That, in my view, is realistic. However, while the markets continue to skyrocket, it's a shame if you're not in the game. You have to be in to win, but you have to be naturally jumpy and get out quickly when things look like they are turning. What keeps the Dow going is the wall of money being thrown at it by the pension funds in America. However, although stock markets are volatile, they are quite easy for the amateur to work out. When interest rates are low, there is nowhere for all the money to go except into stocks, and as interest rates rise, people will sell stocks and go into higher interest-paying bonds, or they will put their money on deposit at the local bank. So if interest rates are creeping up, you'll see the stock markets come down. Easy-peasy-lemon-squeezy, any twit can work that one out.

Now sometimes it happens that you know of an obscure company that has great things in the pipeline and you can make a killing, so I'd never say keep away from stocks altogether. I once made $500,000 in three weeks investing in two obscure mining stocks that had good things happening, but chances like that are few and far between. The stock markets are a rigged casino, designed to take the little guy's money. But like all casinos, you can go in and win. Information is the key, and don't bet the farm and don't buy the story that the share-price con will last forever, for one day all the shareholders in the world will wake up to the conclusion that they are risking a lot of money for very little income, and once there are no greater opportunities up ahead, things will have to correct to what is realistic.

Bonds

The question of whether you should be in bonds depends again largely on what you feel interest rates will do. When interest rates rise, bond values fall, and vice versa. Bonds are generally safer than stocks, and they pay a higher return. Again, you have to guess accurately on inflation and interest rates. The variable is, if people's confidence plunges, and if that affects currencies, then interest rates might have to go up to protect against a run in the foreign exchange markets. Lenders would want to hedge against possible risks, and bonds might fall through the floor. So the question is: What are the governments going to do if there is a crisis? If they desperately need money to sustain themselves and their debt, then interest rates would be forced up, as available lenders would have them over a barrel. Then you have to factor in the bullish effect that people fleeing a falling stock market might have on bonds, as traditionally they go into bonds for yield and safety in times of trouble. Personally, I think the bond market is very hard to call accurately, but paper is still paper, so I would stay out of bonds in a major correction, or even a depression.

The exception is holding government paper like Treasury bills. Of course you have to continue to believe that the government will honor its debts. The government of the USA or Britain may never default—they could just print more cash if the need arises. But they could restructure debt and stall payments, and so on. I would definitely not hold any municipal or corporate bonds, not even the AAA-rated ones—not because the big companies will necessarily default, but because the issuers of bonds pay their obligations by printing and selling more bonds.

If the market loses confidence, who's going to buy the new issue in order for the old bondholders to be settled? In a tight situation, I can see corporations and even governments forcing bondholders to roll over their bonds. Then, although the bondholders would be receiving the interest due, they might not be able to cash out when they wanted to. Further, if the market in bonds is weak, you might have to eat a hell of a loss to get anyone to take your bond.

Why invest in a piece of paper whose value fluctuates. In recent years, many bond prices were adversely affected because of the leveraged buyout (LBO) craze. In an LBO, the incoming buyer loads up the company he is acquiring with massive debt. This affects the value of the current bonds. So people who have lent money to the company in the past find the value of that money depreciating because some wide-eyed kid takes over the company in order to mess around with its assets so he can make a quick hundred million dollars. I don't see any justice in that, and I would not subject my assets to that kind of risk. In a period of deflation, there is no saying what a company will do to stay liquid. Bondholders are always at the whims of those in the boardroom.

Again, if you are into bonds, the prudent move is to hold only a percentage of your assets in government or corporate bonds in case you are ever denied access to that money. As for junk bonds, forget it! That is one market that will be chewed out mercilessly. I might be wrong, but the poor quality and sheer extent of that paper is such that I don't see who would buy the stuff in a depression.

Certificates of Deposit

A better alternative to corporate bonds are certificates of deposit (CDs). CDs don't fluctuate in value: Whatever you put in is what you get out. Almost all of the major banks will survive a correction as governments bail out big banks. It's the smaller banks that may be in trouble. Theoretically, the U.S. government, through the Federal Deposit Insurance Corporation (FDIC), guarantees bank deposits. But if the government were strapped and bank defaults were on the rise, I don't see where the money would come from to settle everyone instantly. Again, I could see the government playing for time and paying people off with either more government paper or, bit by bit, with time payments. So stay away from little banks. Your best bets are large international banks.

I'm not the kind of person who puts money on deposit especially at today's low interest rates. In the past I have been more the *kamikaze* investor: It's all or nothing for me. I have chosen highly speculative foreign stocks in which I was looking to make between 100 percent and 300 percent on the turn. You can't do that in times of contraction. Once interest rates rise, CDs offer a defensive play to the vagaries of the stock market and troubled times. Unexciting, but safe enough.

I think after the millennium, things may get very choppy indeed, and in any correction the game is to defend your assets so that once prices finish falling, you will be able to go back into the market and buy up quality investments at a fraction of their former value. CDs at major international banks might become a good bet in the future if interest rates rise.

Money market accounts offer higher interest rates than do CDs, but the problem is with the paper in which the money market mutual fund has invested. I can see all sorts of problems with money market funds in the coming years. I would opt for safety and stay out of any investment that you don't manage for yourself.

Gold, Silver, and Precious Metals

Because precious metals are linked to inflation, again you are going to have to guess where inflation might go. However, gold and silver are the only two currencies that all the world agrees have real value. If there is any crisis of confidence, people will flood into precious metals regardless of inflation rates.

In recent years, gold has been disempowered by low interest rates, low inflation, and central bank selling. There's no market in gold at today's prices ($314), and there doesn't look like there will much of a market until inflation picks up or until there is a jolly good crisis to rattle everyone's cage. Interestingly enough, very little of the world's gold is in the hands of the small investor. It is mostly held by mining companies, central banks, and the large institutions. If the general public *en masse* tried to go out and buy up gold, supplies would soon dry up. Even though world gold production is rising fast, you have to remember that it is a rare metal, so there is a limit as to how much gold can be produced if everyone wants it suddenly.

South Africa and Russia dominate the gold market. Again, you would have to guess what will happen to these two countries over the next few years. If Russia comes under economic pressure, will it start dumping gold? Or, will social unrest in South Africa close the mines, making gold more scarce? It's impossible to call accurately. But at this time, an ounce of gold costs $250 or more to mine, so I can't see gold going much below about $300, no matter what happens. With almost no downside potential and a huge upside possibility, I would say that gold is an excellent bet. Certainly I would have a substantial part of my portfolio in gold. But I'm a gold freak. I mostly invest in gold and gold shares, and I know that someday, gold will the only game in town. However, that may not happen for five to ten years, and there are other things to buy in the meantime.

Most analysts recommend holding about 5 percent of your portfolio in precious metals. However, the concerted move by governments and the institutions to disempower gold and drive the price down tells you something. They don't like gold, as citizens can buy it and move it around without anyone knowing about it. All the more reason to have some.

Gold stocks are a specialized play, and you have to know what you are doing. My rule is that I try to never buy a gold stock unless I know the guy doing the digging. But right now, gold stocks are at their all-time low, so there are opportunities to be had on a two- or three-year view. If you're into gold stocks, I would choose the Australian mines rather than American, Canadian, or South African. The reason is that Aussie gold mines are cheap compared to other gold shares, and they operate in a politically stable country.

Silver is a different story. Much of it is mined in the Third

World, and if those countries get into a cash crunch, which is likely, they might start dumping silver as a way out of trouble. However, variables affect the silver market like any other, so I wouldn't write it off as an investment, especially in troubled times. It's just that I personally prefer gold.

Pension Plans and Annuities

Pension plans and annuities are usually invested in either real estate or stocks. I could foresee a number of pension funds going down the drain as the investments they have made turn out to be worthless. Some private pension plans are insured by the government, but again, one doesn't know what the government may do if there is a cash crunch. If you have the option of getting your money out of one of these plans, do so. It will be safer in your hands than in the hands of a stranger whose motivations may not have your best interests at heart.

Conclusion

If you see a correction or depression as just energy—the in-breathing and out-breathing of the world mind—you are already on top of it, because you are out of the emotion. The name of the game will be not to allow other people's fears and emotions to throw you off balance. In a world where everyone might be extremely rattled all at once, your chances are strengthened a hundredfold if you don't lose your head. If you plan defensively, or even if you find that there is little you can do, as you don't have a lot of assets, you can still change the way you feel and come from an energy that is the opposite of everyone else's.

In hard times, mediocrity will be taken out at the knees, but excellence always survives. If you start today, make whatever you do "special," and put value and effort into your work, you will not only survive, but also prosper. The first ones to be laid off will be the useless ones. The truly talented, dedicated men and women will be those that industry keeps. So it is only a matter of raising your energy for you to put yourself into a comfortable position whereby no one could afford to lay you off since you are too valuable a cog in the wheel.

Remember, a correction is just a time of well-earned rest. It doesn't have to be a storm. See it as a gift, and use the time offered wisely. Improve yourself, spend more time with your family, strengthen your body, and reappraise your direction in life. See contraction as the gift that saved the world and allowed it to recover. Sure enough, once the world mind agrees that the rest has gone on long enough, things will gradually return to their former pace. When that happens, you will be back in the market with an even greater strength.

Finally, *recession, depression, inflation, correction,* and *stagnation* are terms that describe the official economy. The unofficial economy has a mind of its own. Although car production might be down 25 percent, there will be underground industries that will double overnight. If you are alive to your opportunities and scout around in the marketplace, you will easily find a way of turning a buck or two. Nothing stops. It just moves at a more leisurely pace, or it goes underground.

People tend to think of a depression as a holocaust, a kind of Mad Max landscape of postnuclear proportions. Nothing could be further from the truth. The golden years of American cinema were the 1930s. During the last depression, people who exercised no control over their affairs were wiped out, but others did fantastically well, and their sons and daughters are multimillionaires today. It's only a matter of attitude. Crisis for the masses is opportunity for the individual. Never forget that.

If you are alive and active and are prepared to put out some good energy, you will thrive in volatile markets. The power you discover within will be more than enough to keep you and your loved ones with all their needs met and more. Further, if things downturn, people will be pulled together. They will have to cooperate with each other. The family unit will be strengthened once more, and we will all have to learn to love and tolerate one another. That will be a great victory for humankind. I believe the period of change after the millennium will herald a great awakening, a spiritual renaissance. I'm personally looking forward to it. If you get yourself together and don't lose sight of your quest, you can, too.

About the Author

Author and lecturer **Stuart Wilde** is one of the real characters of the self-help, human potential movement. His style is humorous, controversial, poignant, and transformational. He has written 11 books, including those that make up the very successful Taos Quintet, which are considered classics in their genre. They are: *Affirmations*, *The Force*, *Miracles*, *The Quickening*, and *The Trick to Money Is Having Some!*. Stuart's books have been translated into 12 languages.

Stuart Wilde International Tour and Seminar Information:

For information on Stuart Wilde's latest tour and
seminar dates in the USA and Canada, contact:

White Dove International
P.O. Box 1000, Taos, NM 87571
(505) 758-0500
(505) 758-2265 (fax)

Stuart's Website: **www.powersource.com/wilde**

We hope you enjoyed this Hay House book.
If you would like to receive a free catalog
featuring additional Hay House books and products,
or if you would like information
about the Hay Foundation, please write to:

Hay House, Inc.
P.O. Box 5100
Carlsbad, CA 92018-5100

(800) 654-5126
(800) 650-5115 (fax)

Please visit the Hay House Website at: **www.hayhouse.com**